Edinburgh Law Essentials

SCOTTISH SUCCESSION LAW ESSENTIALS

EDINBURGH LAW ESSENTIALS

Series Editor: Nicholas Grier, Abertay University, Dundee

www.edinburghuniversitypress.com/series/ele

Edinburgh Law Essentials

SCOTTISH SUCCESSION LAW ESSENTIALS

Second edition

Frankie McCarthy and Duncan Adam

EDINBURGH
University Press

Edinburgh University Press is one of the leading university presses in the UK. We publish academic books and journals in our selected subject areas across the humanities and social sciences, combining cutting-edge scholarship with high editorial and production values to produce academic works of lasting importance. For more information visit our website: edinburghuniversitypress.com

Previous edition published in 2013 by Dundee University Press

Edinburgh University Press Ltd
13 Infirmary Street
Edinburgh EH1 1LT

Typeset in 10/13 Bembo by
Deanta Global Publishing Services, Chennai, India

A CIP record for this book is available from the British Library

ISBN 978 1 3995 3597 7 (hardback)
ISBN 978 1 3995 3598 4 (paperback)
ISBN 978 1 3995 3599 1 (webready PDF)
ISBN 978 1 3995 3600 4 (epub)

CONTENTS

TABLE OF CASES

LIST OF ABBREVIATIONS

1964 Act	Succession (Scotland) Act 1964
Hiram, *Succession*	H Hiram, *The Scots Law of Succession* (2nd ed, 2007)
Macdonald, *Succession*	DR Macdonald, *Succession* (3rd ed, 2001)

GLOSSARY

Beneficiary   A person receiving property under a testamentary writing or on intestacy

Codicil   An extra piece of writing added on to a will at a later date

Declarator   A type of court order which declares a factual situation to exist, e.g. declarator of marriage, declarator of death

Decree   The final decision by the judge in a court case

Estate   All the property someone owns. It includes intangible things like rights and debts as well as tangible assets and money

Executor   A person responsible for ingathering and distributing the deceased's estate. In the book, this term is gender neutral, although historically the term 'executrix' has been used to refer to a female executor

Exr/Exrx   Abbreviation of 'executor' or 'executrix'

Intestate   Without a will

Issue   Children, grandchildren and any further generations of descendants

Judicial factor   Someone appointed by the court to take care of the affairs of another person who is no longer able to make decisions for him or herself, e.g. because of illness

Jus relicti/relictae   The common law right held by a surviving spouse or civil partner of the deceased to payment of certain sums from the deceased's estate

Legacy   An item, object, sum of money, etc., left to a beneficiary in a will

Legatee   The recipient or beneficiary of a legacy

Legitim   The common law right held by any surviving children of the deceased to payment of certain sums from the deceased's estate. Also known as 'legal rights'

Next-of-kin   No formal legal meaning, but usually used to mean a person's spouse or civil partner and/or the nearest blood relative(s) based on the hierarchy of relations in the Succession (Scotland) Act 1964, s2

Testament   Any deed that creates and gives effect to a person's intentions as to the disposal of her property after death. Sometimes referred to as a testamentary disposition

Testator   A person making a testamentary writing. In the book, this term is gender neutral, although historically the term 'testatrix' has been used to refer to a female testator

Tr/Trs   Abbreviations of trustee and trustees

Will   The most common type of testamentary writing

1 INTRODUCTION

The law of succession regulates what happens to a person's property when they die. It is an area of law which will almost certainly affect us all. Rules of succession are found in the earliest legal records in Scotland, and some of the principles established as long ago as the fourteenth century continue to resonate in the law today. Different rationales can be suggested for the system of rules now in place, but an overriding concern has always been to distribute the property of the deceased in the way they would have wanted. The law will usually try to give effect to the deceased's wishes whether they made a will or not.

In most universities, succession is taught alongside property law. In practice, succession questions frequently also involve family law, contract law and certain aspects of public law such as tax and citizenship rules. It is difficult for a practitioner in any area of private law to avoid succession entirely. Law students may also find succession an area in which family and friends have a keen interest based on events in their own lives. A good grasp of the basics is essential.

As with most areas of private law in Scotland, succession rules are drawn from a variety of sources. The intestacy framework (the law which applies when a deceased person has not made a will) was overhauled by the Succession (Scotland) Act 1964, which has been repeatedly amended subsequently to keep pace with changes in society. The Succession (Scotland) Act 2016 clarified some aspects of testate succession (where the deceased person *has* made a will) and reformed the law of survivorship, amongst other things. Case law and customary law remain important, more so than in many other areas of private law.

Further reform to the law of succession in the short or medium term seems likely. The Scottish Government has conducted a number of public consultations over the past ten years on potential changes. Although many are critical of the status quo, there is little consensus on what an improved system should look like, and the government continues to work on developing proposals that will command the support of a majority of the population. The final chapter of the book looks at potential future reforms in more detail.

PROPERTY: GENERAL RULES

The rules of succession deal with distribution of the deceased's 'estate'. The estate is composed of all property in the deceased's **patrimony** at the time of their death. A person's patrimony contains anything with a financial value that the person owns or has some other legal right to, such as a right to be paid money under a contract. The person with responsibility for distributing the estate is known as the executor, discussed further in Chapter 2.

A distinction is drawn in Scots law between **heritable property** and **moveable property**. The distinction is significant for succession law since certain inheritance claims can be made over moveable property but not heritable and vice versa. Heritable property, also known as heritage or immoveable property, describes land and buildings. Anything which has become attached to heritage, like trees in a garden, or a central heating system in a house, will also be regarded as heritage under the law of fixtures. Hereditary titles ('the Marquis of Breadalbane') and coats of arms also fall within this category, although these are encountered infrequently in practice. A final, more complex, example is any right having 'a tract of future time', meaning a right that can continue to be exercised on an ongoing basis into the future. A lease of a flat fits this definition, as does the right to payment of annuity.

Moveable property covers everything which is not heritage, including corporeal moveable items – those with a tangible physical presence, like a car or a table – and incorporeal moveable items such as money in a bank account or shares in a company. Personal rights, such as the right to payment of money arising under a contract, are also moveable property.

It is not usually difficult to determine which of the two categories a given piece of property will fall into, although more detailed discussion of the potential complexities can be found in KGC Reid,

'Property', in *The Laws of Scotland: Stair Memorial Encyclopedia*, volume 18 (1993), paragraphs 11–16.

Whether property is heritable or moveable will be determined as at the date and time of the deceased's death. In a limited number of cases, property can be converted from one category to the other for the purposes of distributing the estate. Imagine that the deceased was in the process of selling their house. At the time of death, they had agreed a contract of sale (known as 'missives') with a buyer, but had yet to deliver to them the deed of transfer (known as the 'disposition') or receive the purchase price in exchange. The house therefore remains in the deceased's patrimony, but is subject to the terms of the sale contract under which it must be transferred to the buyer. In these circumstances, the house would be considered as heritage with a value of zero. The right against the buyer for payment of the purchase price would be moveable property.

Conversion may also be constructive, where a testator has left instructions in their will that the executor should sell property in one category in order to acquire property in the other category for distribution.

Property will not form part of the estate where it involves *delectus personae*, meaning it can be enjoyed only by the specific person who acquired it. This arises in relation to certain types of leases, particularly residential leases, and may also be relevant in respect of contractual rights held against another person such as in a contract of employment.

'Digital assets', such as social media accounts, digital documents and photographs, and online gaming profiles, are increasingly important in modern life, but their position on death is unclear. The existing law of property and succession is poorly adapted to deal with assets of this kind. It is understood the Scottish Government is considering modernising legislation in this area, though the likely content of this legislation or the timescale for its introduction is unclear. Matters are complicated by the fact that most digital content is hosted by a third-party platform which is likely to have its own contractual rules about the treatment of the content on the death of the user. At present, since little can be said with certainty about the treatment of such assets in succession law, the living may be best advised to take the practical steps required to ensure a person they trust can access their digital assets in the event of their death. This would include leaving a note of relevant passwords or security information somewhere accessible by a person they trust after their death.

PERSONS: WHO CAN INHERIT?

The property of a deceased person will be distributed based on the rules discussed in later chapters. The applicable rules will depend on various factors, most significantly the type of property in question and whether or not the deceased has made a will. However, some general rules apply in determining which persons are entitled to inherit property from a deceased.

The first rule is that only living persons may inherit. A person may not receive property from the deceased's estate unless they have outlived the deceased. This is sometimes expressed by saying that survival is a condition of inheritance.

Children

Children are provided with certain default entitlements on the death of a parent (discussed in Chapter 4) and will often be expressly provided for in a parent's will. In the succession context, a child is any person in respect of whom the deceased was legally recognised as a parent. It is not relevant whether the child's parents were married. Historically the concept of 'illegitimate' children (those born outside marriage) was important in succession law, but the last vestiges of this doctrine were abolished by section 21 of the Family Law (Scotland) Act 2006.

Adopted children are recognised as the children of their adoptive parents and not of any other person under sections 23 and 24 of the 1964 Act. An adopted child therefore has no default entitlement in succession following the death of their biological parent, although there is nothing to prevent that parent making provision for the child in their will. Somewhat bizarrely, section 24(1A) of the 1964 Act provides that where the relative ages of siblings are important for rights of succession based on seniority, an adopted person is to be treated as if born on the date of the adoption order. There have been calls for this provision to be repealed.

A child may be born subsequent to the death of their parent, described in law as a 'posthumous child'. In this situation, the child whilst still *in utero* is treated as already having been born for the purposes of succession. The child must survive birth before they are able to acquire ownership or any other legal right in respect of inherited property, since birth is the point at which legal capacity begins.

A child may also be posthumously *conceived* where gametes (sperm or eggs) frozen by a person prior to their death are subsequently used in fertility treatment, or where fertility treatment which began before a person's death results after their death in the successful transfer of an embryo into their partner's womb. Sections 39, 40 and 46 of the Human Fertilisation and Embryology Act 2008 allow for a man whose sperm has been used posthumously in the conception of a child, or any person whose female partner posthumously conceived as a result of treatment which started prior to the death, to be registered as a parent on the birth certificate in certain circumstances. (Posthumous conception of a child using a frozen egg is not a basis on which a donor can be registered as a parent.) No rights in succession follow from birth registration in this case. However, a person is free to make provision for any posthumously conceived child in their will.

Stepchildren do not fall within the definition of 'children' for the purposes of succession law. The same is true of children 'accepted as a child of the family' in the terminology of the Family Law (Scotland) Act 1985, meaning children in respect of whom an adult or adults in the house have taken responsibility despite the absence of a formal legal relationship which requires them to do so. This most commonly occurs where a parent's new partner takes responsibility for children who pre-date that relationship. Stepchildren and 'accepted' children have no automatic entitlement to inherit from their stepparent or *de facto* parent, although of course relevant provision may be made in the stepparent or *de facto* parent's will. The exclusion of stepchildren and accepted children from the meaning of that term in the law of succession is arguably out of step with their position in family law. However, consultation by the Scottish Government has produced no clear consensus on whether or how the law should be reformed here.

Spouses, civil partners and cohabitants

Adult relationships in Scotland may be legally formalised through marriage or civil partnership. The law of succession does not distinguish between these different institutions. For the sake of brevity, **reference to marriage or divorce within this book is accordingly intended to include registration and dissolution of civil partnership**, and reference to a spouse is intended to include reference to a civil partner.

A surviving spouse has an automatic entitlement to inherit from their deceased husband or wife. This entitlement does not arise if the persons have divorced prior to the death but remains in place if they have merely separated. Where a person makes provision for their spouse in their will, that provision will usually be deemed revoked by divorce, discussed further in Chapter 7. Where a cohabiting relationship is brought to an end by the death of one of the cohabitants, the survivor has no automatic entitlement to inherit but may make a claim against the deceased estate under section 29 of the Family Law (Scotland) Act 2006. This is discussed in detail in Chapter 5.

Unworthy heirs

Where a person unlawfully kills another, they are deemed an 'unworthy heir' and forfeit any rights they may have held to succeed to their victim's estate. This common law rule was modified by section 17 of the Succession (Scotland) Act 2016 which provides that the offender should be treated as having predeceased their victim for the purposes of succession. Section 2 of the Forfeiture Act 1982 provides the court with a discretion to modify the effect of this rule on application by the offender, with an amendment by section 15 of the Succession (Scotland) Act 2016 empowering the court to exclude the rule entirely 'where the justice of the case so requires'. Section 5 of the 1982 Act provides that an application for modification of the rule cannot be made by a person who has been convicted of murder, restricting the scope of the Act in Scotland to those convicted of culpable homicide.

DEBTS

The deceased's debts must be paid from the estate before any claims in succession can be satisfied. Certain debts are privileged, meaning they must be paid before others. Deathbed and funeral expenses rank first. If they are paid in full, next in line are arrears of tax and social security, and payment of wages to employees for up to four months prior to the death. Once those are paid in full, all other creditors have an equal claim on the estate. If there are insufficient funds to cover all the debts, each creditor will receive an equal percentage of what they were owed by the deceased.

A creditor who holds a right in security in one or more items of the deceased's property is in a different position from ordinary creditors. A secured creditor may exercise their rights under the security to recoup what they are owed, usually by selling the property over which the security is held. Where the security is held over a building or plot of land (colloquially referred to as a mortgage, but properly known as a heritable security or standard security), the debt which it secures will be considered a heritable debt, recorded in the inventory of the estate as a burden on the building or plot of land in question. Heritable debts must be paid from the heritage in the estate. Moveable debts, which include debts secured on moveable property as well as all unsecured debts, must be paid from the moveables in the estate. If two securities exist in respect of the same debt, one held over heritage and one held over moveable property, the proportion secured over heritage should be paid from heritage, and the proportion secured over moveables paid from moveables.

Family members of the deceased may be able to claim financial support, known as aliment, from the estate. Section 1 of the Family Law (Scotland) Act 1985 provides that a person must, during their lifetime, aliment their spouse and also aliment their children until the age of 18, or the age of 25 if the children are in full-time education or training. A person to whom this duty was owed immediately before the death can claim temporary aliment from the estate if necessary to cover their financial needs during the period between the death and the distribution of the estate. If the distribution of the estate does not leave them adequately provided for, they may also claim continuing support for as long as necessary from the beneficiaries of the estate, known as aliment *ex jure representationis*. Claims of either type are rare. Aliment is considered a debt on the estate, to be paid after the debts of ordinary creditors have been satisfied.

If the debts on the estate significantly exceed the assets, the estate can be subject to sequestration (bankruptcy). In such a situation, the expenses arising from the sequestration will be paid before any other debt including funeral expenses. Information on the sequestration procedure can be found on the website of the Accountant in Bankruptcy (www.aib.gov.uk).

INHERITANCE TAX

When a person dies, the property in their estate becomes liable to inheritance tax (IHT). The rules on IHT are set out in the Inheritance Tax Act 1984, updated by various Finance Acts. (A Finance Act is passed every year to implement the changes set out by the Chancellor of the Exchequer in the Budget.) IHT is a large and complex subject which cannot be explored in depth here. Certain aspects of succession law are difficult to grasp without a basic understanding of IHT, however, and so the bare bones of the system are set out here.

Inheritance tax is charged on the total value of the property in the estate at the point of death together with any property transferred out of the estate in the seven years immediately preceding the death. This latter rule is to prevent people avoiding IHT by disposing of all their assets shortly before they die. All property in Scotland is subject to IHT, and all property outside Scotland owned by a person domiciled in Scotland is also liable.

Tax is charged at 0% up to a threshold amount, currently £325,000. This means that where the total assets amount to less than £325,000, no tax is paid. Most intestate estates in Scotland fall within this limit. Any property exceeding the threshold is taxed at 40% of its value. For example, imagine the total assets are worth £400,000. The first £325,000 is charged at 0%. The remaining £75,000 is charged at 40%. The tax due will therefore be £30,000.

The IHT regime includes a number of exemptions. No tax has to be paid in respect of property transferred to the deceased's spouse on death or in the preceding seven years. The same is true of property given to charities or certain other protected beneficiaries, such as political parties. Some types of property, usually of historical or cultural interest, are exempt where they are available for public access. Tax relief is also provided for certain types of business property and for transfers in quick succession, amongst other things.

It is common for people with substantial assets to take advice on how to make the most of these exemptions in order to minimise the amount of inheritance tax to be paid on their death. This is referred to as 'executry planning' or 'executry tax planning'. Succession cases are sometimes easier to understand in the knowledge that the provisions of a will or decisions taken by the parties involved may have been motivated by the tax consequences.

Responsibility for valuing the estate and ensuring tax is paid rests with the executor. Payment must normally be made within six months of the date of death. In practice, inheritance tax is always the first debt on the estate to be paid, since the executor will not be confirmed until this happens.

Further information on inheritance tax can be found on the UK Government website at www.gov.uk/inheritance-tax.

INTERNATIONAL PRIVATE LAW

Complications arise where the deceased is a Scottish person living in Scotland who owns property in another part of the world, or where the deceased is a person living elsewhere in the world who owns property in Scotland.

Where the deceased is Scottish, moveable property will always be dealt with under the Scots law of succession, regardless of where the property is to be found in the world. Heritage, however, will be dealt with by the *lex situs* – the law governing the place where the property is located.

Where the deceased is domiciled elsewhere, but has left property in Scotland, questions of succession are likely to be regulated by an agreement between the UK and the jurisdiction in question, although the type of property involved may also influence the outcome.

For a detailed account of the IPL rules, see EB Crawford and JM Carruthers, *International Private Law: A Scots Perspective* (4th ed, 2015), chapter 18.

Essential facts

- The law of succession sets out the rules on what happens to a person's property after death.

- The estate is made up of all the property in the deceased person's patrimony on death.

- Property can be heritable (land and buildings) or moveable (everything else.) Certain succession rules will only affect heritable property, whilst others will only affect moveable property.

- A person must survive the deceased in order to inherit property from the deceased's estate.

- Children of the deceased will include adopted children and children *in utero* at the time of the death. It will not include stepchildren or accepted children.

- Debts, including inheritance tax, are the first thing to be paid from the estate. If the deceased had more debts than assets, no-one will receive an inheritance.

FURTHER READING

Hiram, *Succession*, chapter 2

Macdonald, *Succession*, chapters 2–3 and 14–15

R Paisley, "The succession rights of the unborn child" (2006) 10(1) Edin LR 29

KGC Reid, MJ de Waal and R Zimmermann (eds), *Exploring the Law of Succession* (2007)

2 DEATH, THE BODY AND SURVIVORSHIP

DEATH

Succession involves the transfer of property on death from the patrimony of one person to the patrimony of another person. It follows that the starting point for the operation of the law of succession generally requires one person to die and another person to survive. Usually determining whether a person is dead or alive is a straightforward question of medical fact. Complications may arise, however, when people die together in circumstances where it proves impossible to determine the order in which their deaths occurred.

When a person has died, the Registration of Births, Deaths and Marriages (Scotland) Act 1965 provides that a physician must issue a certificate of death specifying the cause of death (section 24), which must be registered with the District Registrar within eight days of death or of discovering the body (section 23). If the circumstances of the death are unusual or suspicious, the procurator fiscal will conduct enquiries which may lead to a postmortem or a public inquiry.

Where a person is missing and thought to be dead, but their body has not been found, an application to the court to have the person declared dead may be made under the Presumption of Death (Scotland) Act 1977. The court will grant the declarator if it is satisfied, on the balance of probabilities, that the person is either dead or has not been known to be alive for at least seven years. The first test would likely be satisfied where, for example, a boat has sunk far from land and no survivors can be found – a person who was on the boat is more likely to be dead than alive. In that sort of case, section 2 provides that the court will fix the date of death as being the last day on which the person might, as a matter of proof, have been thought to be alive.

The second test would be relevant where, for example, a healthy person has simply disappeared, and no evidence is available to suggest that they have died rather than simply moving elsewhere to begin a new life. In this situation, section 2 provides that the date of death will be the day occurring seven years after the person was last known to be alive.

Section 3 provides that a declarator by the court under the 1977 Act has the same effect as a certificate of death, meaning that the law of succession will operate. If the missing person was married, that relationship is dissolved, and will not revive should it later transpire that the missing person is still alive. The declarator does not, however, absolve the missing person of responsibility for any criminal offences, whether committed before or after the declarator is granted.

It is possible to apply to the court to have the declarator varied (if further evidence becomes available about the circumstances of the death) or recalled (if the missing person turns out to be alive). Where the declarator resulted in any person acquiring rights in the missing person's property, recall of the declarator will not affect those rights unless the court thinks it is fair and reasonable to make an order providing otherwise. An application for such an order must be made within five years of the date of the declarator. Sections 5 and 6 of the 1977 Act impose upon the executor a duty to take out insurance when distributing an estate on the basis of a declarator of death in case the declarator is later recalled and an order made varying property rights acquired in the deceased's property as a result.

THE BODY

No-one has a right of ownership over the body of the deceased, which is in the custody of the executor until disposal by burial, cremation or any other method. To determine what form of disposal is appropriate, often the deceased will have made an 'arrangements on death declaration', typically in their will, expressing a wish about what should happen to their body when they die. Where they have not expressed any wish, section 65 of the Burial and Cremation (Scotland) Act 2016 provides that it is the nearest relative as defined in the Act who is entitled to decide. The Act also regulates burials and cremations more generally. If no-one else has done so, the local authority has responsibility to arrange for disposal of the body as per sections 50(1) and (6) of the National Assistance Act 1948. Any person making payment for funeral expenses has a right to be repaid from the deceased's estate.

SURVIVORSHIP

Since a dead person cannot inherit, the order in which people die can be significant in the law of succession. Imagine that Anna and Bert are friends, each of whom has made a will leaving their entire estate to the other. If Anna dies first, Bert will inherit her estate. On Bert's death, his whole estate, including the possessions he has inherited from Anna, will go to someone else. However, if Bert dies first, Anna will inherit his estate, with the property going elsewhere on Anna's death.

Normally, there will be no difficulty in establishing who died first. Sometimes things are less clear, for example where several people are killed in an event like a car crash. Such a circumstance is referred to as a common calamity. Where it is impossible to ascertain the order of deaths as a matter of fact, section 9 of the Succession (Scotland) Act 2016 (replacing earlier, more complicated, rules) provides that each person is to be treated as having failed to survive the others. Returning to Anna and Bert, imagine that each has the same will described previously, but that both die in a crash. Medics cannot determine the time of death for either person. Since they died in a common calamity and the order of deaths is unknown, section 9 applies. Neither is deemed to have survived the other. Anna cannot inherit Bert's estate because she has not survived him, and so his estate will pass elsewhere as provided for in his will or under the rules of intestate succession. Similarly, Bert cannot inherit Anna's estate which will also pass elsewhere.

Essential facts

- When a person dies, the rules of succession will begin to operate.
- When a person dies, it is necessary for their death to be registered.

- The Presumption of Death (Scotland) Act 1977 allows for a declarator of death to be granted by a court where a person dies but no body can be found or where they have been missing for at least seven years. A declarator triggers the succession rules in the same way as a death certificate.

- For succession purposes, where two or more people die in a common calamity, none of the people who die is deemed to have survived the other(s).

FURTHER READING

Hiram, *Succession*, chapter 1
Macdonald, *Succession*, chapter 1

3 EXECUTORS AND THE ADMINISTRATION OF THE ESTATE

The executor is the person responsible for ingathering the deceased's estate, paying their debts and distributing legacies to the beneficiaries. Any person aged 16 or over may act as an executor. Where the deceased has left a will, it is common for two or more executors to act together. The office is gratuitous, meaning there is no entitlement to remuneration, unless specific testamentary provision has been made by the deceased to that effect.

An executor-nominate is a person nominated for the role by the deceased in the will. Where the deceased has not named anyone, or where the person nominated refuses or is unable to act, the Executors (Scotland) Act 1900 provides alternatives. In the unlikely event that the deceased has named a trustee in the will, but not an executor, that person will be deemed to have been nominated also as executor. A general disponee, universal legatee or residuary legatee (see the discussion in Chapter 7) will also be deemed to have been nominated. If more than one person fulfils these conditions, they can act jointly. Any person nominated either expressly or under the 1900 Act has the option to decline the office.

Where there is no executor-nominate, usually because there is no will, someone must petition the sheriff to be appointed in the role. An executor obtaining office through this process is known as an executor-dative. The law sets out an order of preference as to who is entitled to be appointed. If the deceased is survived by a spouse, and the estate will be exhausted by the spouse's prior rights claim (see the discussion in Chapter 4), the spouse is top of the list for appointment according to current practice. Relatives of the deceased are otherwise entitled to be appointed in the same order in which they are entitled to inherit under section 2 of the Succession (Scotland) Act 1964, discussed in detail in Chapter 5. If no executor can be found from these categories, next in line will be creditors of the deceased, then legatees, and finally the procurator fiscal or a judicial factor. If more than one person in a particular category seeks to take on the role, they will be appointed as joint executors.

At present, the court cannot refuse to appoint a person as executor-dative unless another person in a preferred category is competing for the office. However, section 21 of the Succession (Scotland) Act 2016 allows the Scottish Ministers to make regulations imposing conditions on the appointment of executors-dative. Regulations might, for example, require the court to be satisfied that the proposed executor-dative is a suitable person to be appointed an executor. No regulations have been made to date.

The executor must determine the extent of the deceased's assets and liabilities, before following the procedure for obtaining confirmation to the estate. Confirmation is the court order which gives the executor legal title to deal with the deceased's assets and is obtained from the Sheriff Court. The application process for confirmation requires the executor to complete a form known as a C1, which includes an inventory listing all the property in the deceased's estate and its value. Property should be included whether it is located in Scotland or elsewhere. The law does not specify the form in which the inventory must be prepared or the circumstances in which a professional valuation of property (as opposed to the executor's reasonable estimate) must be acquired. Conventions tend to apply as a matter of legal practice, however. More detail can be found in Macdonald, *Succession*, paragraphs 13.29–13.44.

Where inheritance tax will be payable (and in some cases even if no inheritance tax is payable), the executor must also complete an inheritance tax form. If inheritance tax is payable, the provisional amount of tax will be calculated on the basis of the inventory and this must be paid by the executor before the court will issue confirmation.

To obtain confirmation, the executor must submit the C1 form and inventory to the sheriff clerk. An executor-nominate, in addition to the inventory, must lodge a copy of the will naming them as executor. At present, the court cannot refuse to confirm an executor-nominate, though it has been suggested that the court should have the power to do so where the proposed executor-nominate is unsuited to the office.

An executor-dative, in addition to the inventory, is required to lodge a bond of caution (pronounced 'kayshun'), which is a financial guarantee that 'they will make the estate forthcoming' – in other words, that they will distribute the assets to the beneficiaries. Caution is usually provided in the form of an insurance policy, meaning that if the executor does embezzle from the estate, the beneficiaries will receive compensation from the insurer. It is not necessary for caution to be lodged where the executor is the surviving spouse inheriting the entire estate in prior rights, following section 5 of the Law Reform (Miscellaneous Provisions) (Scotland) Act 1985. The Scottish Law Commission has argued that the requirement to find caution places a disproportionate financial and administrative burden on the executor and recommended that it should be abolished (Report on the Law of Succession (2009), paragraphs 7.6–7.12). Section 19(1) of the Succession (Scotland) Act 2016 empowers the Scottish Ministers to make regulations removing the requirement for caution in certain circumstances. No regulations have been made to date.

When confirmation is granted, it is the executor's proof to other parties that they have legal title to deal with the estate assets. If the executor subsequently discovers assets which were not included within the inventory for confirmation, they must produce a corrective inventory and pay additional inheritance tax due (if any). The executor will then be granted an 'eik' (pronounced 'eek') to their confirmation which includes the newly discovered property. Should an executor deal with assets without confirmation, this is known as vitious intromission with the estate, and may result in the executor becoming personally liable for any debts owed by the deceased.

Once confirmation has been issued, the executor can begin ingathering the deceased's assets and paying their debts. The executor has an obligation to pay any debts of which they become aware so long as there are funds in the estate to do so. Creditors, unless they hold a right in security, must make their claims within six months of the death in order to be paid (or to receive a percentage should the estate turn out to be insolvent). Creditors' claims made after the six-month period should be paid if there are remaining funds. The practical effect of these rules is that the executor cannot start distributing legacies to the beneficiaries until after the six months have passed, unless they are

very sure that there are no debts outstanding. If the executor distributes the estate within six months, and a claim is subsequently made
by a creditor, the executor may become personally liable for that debt.

When debts are paid, the executor then distributes the estate to
the beneficiaries under the will or following the rules of intestate
succession. At the stage of the final distribution, after payment of any
outstanding inheritance tax, the beneficiaries are entitled to see a full
account of the executor's dealings. At this point, the executor should
seek a discharge from the beneficiaries, by which they acknowledge
that they have received what is due to them from the estate and that
there can be no further challenge to the executor's intromissions with
the estate. This will not prevent a beneficiary from making a claim for
breach of trust if it is subsequently discovered that the executor has
acted outwith their powers.

The procedure is different if the estate is a small estate. A small
estate is currently defined as one where the value does not exceed
£36,000 prior to deduction of debts and funeral expenses. The value
is increased from time to time by statutory instrument to take account
of inflation. In the case of a small estate, a simplified procedure is
available and, where an executor-dative is required, there is no need
for a separate application for their appointment. Instead, the sheriff
clerk assists an uncontested executor to complete the C1 form and
the inventory and the other formalities. Section 18 of the Succession
(Scotland) Act 2016 removed the requirement for an executor to find
caution when following the small estate procedure.

EXECUTOR AS TRUSTEE

The executor of an estate is also a trustee. A trust is a legal concept in
which one person, called the trustee, owns property which they are
only allowed to use for the benefit of specific persons or categories
of people, known as beneficiaries. The easiest way to understand the
concept of a trust in Scotland is to imagine that the trustee has two
patrimonies. The first is the trustee's personal patrimony, containing
their personal assets which they can use or dispose of as they please.
The second is the trust patrimony, containing trust assets which can
only be used for the beneficiaries. Instructions on how, and for whose

benefit, trust assets should be used are given by the truster, meaning the person who placed the assets into the trust patrimony in the first place. Since the trust property is held in a separate patrimony, any difficulties affecting the trustee's personal patrimony – for example, if the trustee becomes bankrupt – have no effect on the trust property. The trustee's personal creditors cannot make claims on property in the trust patrimony.

In the context of succession, the truster is the deceased. The trustee is the executor, and the content of the trust patrimony is the property in the estate. The executor-trustee may only administer the property for the good of the beneficiaries, namely the deceased's heirs under the will or under the rules of intestacy.

Since the executor is a trustee, the general law of trusts applies to their dealings with the estate. In particular, the trustee is in a fiduciary relationship with the beneficiaries, meaning that the trustee must take reasonable care in how they deal with the trust property and will be liable to the beneficiaries if they do not live up to that standard. The Trusts and Succession (Scotland) Act 2024 includes a list of the trustee's powers and responsibilities, although the basic fiduciary nature of the role remains. Detailed information on the law of trusts can be found in GL Gretton and AJM Steven, *Property, Trusts and Succession* (2021) chapters 23, 24 and 25.

Essential facts

- The executor is the person responsible for investigating, ingathering and then distributing the deceased's estate.
- The deceased may name an executor in the will, known as an executor-nominate.
- If there is no executor-nominate, usually because there is no will, an executor-dative is appointed by the court. An executor-dative is usually the deceased's closest living relative.
- The executor prepares an inventory of the estate, then seeks a court order called confirmation based on the inventory. Confirmation gives the executor legal title to deal with the property.

- The executor pays the deceased's debts and distributes all remaining property in the estate to the beneficiaries.
- The executor is a trustee in respect of the contents of the estate.

FURTHER READING

JG Currie, *Confirmation of Executors* (9th ed by EM Scobie, 2011)
Macdonald, *Succession*, chapter 13

4 LEGAL RIGHTS

A surviving spouse and any surviving child of a deceased person have an indefeasible entitlement to inherit a share of their estate. This entitlement, known somewhat confusingly as 'legal rights', arises automatically on the deceased's death. Legal rights can be claimed regardless of whether the estate is testate or intestate. In other words, it is not possible for the deceased to disinherit their spouse or children. Where legal rights are claimed on a testate estate, satisfying those claims may have the result that there are insufficient funds left in the estate to pay the legacies in full. In that sense, the deceased's spouse and children are preferred to other intended beneficiaries.

Legal rights have been recognised in the common law of Scotland since before records began. When civil partnership was introduced throughout the UK in 2004, the legal rights of surviving spouses were extended to surviving civil partners. Although various potential reforms to the legal rights regime have been discussed in recent times, it is not clear if or when any changes will occur. This issue is considered further in Chapter 11.

ENTITLEMENT

Legal rights can be claimed only over the moveable property in the estate. Moveable property disposed of by way of a will substitute, discussed in Chapter 8, will not form part of the estate and therefore cannot be subject to legal rights claims.

A surviving spouse is known in law as the relict. The relict's entitlement to legal rights is known as *jus relicti* (for a widower) or *jus relictae* (for a widow). For a surviving civil partner, reference is usually made simply to rights under section 131 of the Civil Partnership Act 2004. In this chapter, references to *jus relictae* should be read to include *jus relicti* and rights under section 131.

The relict is entitled to one-third of the deceased's moveable estate if the deceased is survived by children, or to one-half of the moveable estate if there are no children. The relict must have survived the deceased, and remained married to them at the point of death, or no legal rights entitlement will arise. Imagine Eve dies, leaving behind moveable estate of £9,000. If she has children, her husband Fred will be entitled to one-third of the moveable estate, amounting to £3,000. If she has no children, Fred will be entitled to half the moveable estate amounting to £4,500.

The legal rights of children of the deceased are known as legitim. As discussed in Chapter 1, the definition of children includes posthumous children and adopted children, but not step-children of the deceased. Entitlement to legitim is not restricted to young or dependent children, and in practice legitim payments to adult children are far more common. The legitim fund is made up of one-third of the moveable estate if the deceased has left behind a spouse, or one-half of the moveable estate if there is no spouse. If there is more than one child, the legitim fund will be shared equally between them, known as *per capita* division. Imagine George dies, leaving behind moveable estate of £9,000. If he is survived by a spouse and children, the legitim fund will be £3,000. His three children, Hilary, Ian and Jack, will each receive an equal share of the fund amounting to £1,000 each. If George has no spouse, the legitim fund will be £4,500. This will again be divided equally amongst the children, with each receiving £1,500.

Section 11 of the 1964 Act provides for representation in legitim. This means that, where a child predeceases their parent, their entitlement to legitim is passed down to their own children (the deceased's grandchildren). Representation is infinite, meaning if the grandchildren have also died before the deceased, great-grandchildren can inherit in their place, and so on through the generations. Where representation operates, the grandchildren will be entitled to claim only what their parent would have received from the estate. Where legitim is distributed between descendants of different degrees of relationship to the deceased in this way, it is known as *per stirpes* division of the legitim fund. Look again at the example above of George, who has died leaving £9,000 of moveable estate. He is not survived by a spouse. The youngest of his three children, Jack, died before him, leaving behind twin daughters, Jennifer and Jill. As before, the legitim fund will be £4,500. As before, Hilary and Ian will each receive £1,500 as their share of the fund. The remaining £1,500, which would have gone to Jack, will be shared by his daughters, who will each receive £750 accordingly.

COLLATION

The law assumes that a parent intends to treat each of their children equally. Accordingly, if the parent during their lifetime gives a gift to one child but not to the child's siblings, it is assumed that the gift is an advance payment of the child's legitim. The advance must therefore be taken into account when legitim is distributed following the parent's death. This is known as collation *inter liberos* (meaning 'amongst the children').

The collation principle has its basis in common law and has been expressly preserved by section 11(3) of the 1964 Act. For collation to operate, in the first place a collatable advance must have been received by one (or more) of the legitim claimants. Regular payments made in the discharge of parental duties, such as for food, clothing or school fees, will not meet this test. What is required is a gift that goes beyond the norm. Hiram gives the examples of setting a child up in business or furnishing their home (para 3.10). A gift of heritage cannot be collatable: legitim cannot be claimed from heritable property, and so a gift of heritage cannot be seen as an advance payment of legitim. A loan given by a parent to their child should be distinguished from a collatable advance, since the child will be under an express obligation to repay this money to the estate as part of the original agreement with the parent: the doctrine of collation is not required to make the money liable to repayment.

Collation operates by notionally adding the value of the advance to the existing legitim fund. The overall fund is split between the legitim claimants following the usual rules. The child who has received the advance then takes their share of the legitim fund minus the amount they have already received in the form of the advance.

As an example, the siblings Hilary, Ian and Jack above were each entitled to an equal share in the legitim fund of £4,500, meaning they received £1,500 each. Now, imagine Hilary had received a collatable advance of £600 from her father during his lifetime. This advance is considered part of the legitim fund, increasing the fund's value from £4,500 to £5,100. The fund should be split equally between the three children, entitling them to £1,700 each. Ian and Jack will each receive £1,700. Hilary has already received £600 of her £1,700 share in legitim, so she will receive a payment of £1,100. Each of the children has therefore received £1,700 in legitim. Ian and Jack received the full amount on their father's death. Hilary received £600 during her father's lifetime and the remaining £1,100 on his death.

In the example above, the advance paid to Hilary was less than her eventual entitlement to legitim. Had the advance exceeded her entitlement, she may have been required to pay money back into the legitim fund at the time of her father's death.

It should be noted that collation does not operate automatically. Two caveats apply. In the first place, the child who has received the advance must be called on to collate by their siblings. This may not happen if, for example, the siblings were not aware that any advance had been paid. Secondly, a child who does not claim legal rights cannot be made to collate. Accordingly, a child who has received significant advances of legitim during their parent's lifetime should renounce any claim to legal rights if they wish to maximise their financial reward from the estate.

EXTINGUISHING LEGAL RIGHTS

Legal rights can be extinguished through satisfaction, renunciation or prescription.

Legal rights will be satisfied where their value is paid to the claimant by the executor of the estate. Once payment has been received, it is not possible for the claimant to change their mind and renounce their rights.

Legal rights can be renounced by the claimant. If the renunciation occurs prior to the death of the deceased, the estate including any other legal rights claims will be distributed as if the renouncing claimant had never existed (*Hog v Hog* (1791) Mor 8193). This is because rights renounced prior to the deceased's death have not yet vested in the claimant. (Vesting is discussed in Chapter 9.) As an example, where a widow renounces her claim to *jus relictae* prior to the death of her husband, the legitim fund on his death will be half of the moveable estate in the same way as if he had had no spouse. In legal terminology, the widow's share accresces (meaning 'is added to') to the legitim fund.

In the more common case, renunciation of legal rights will not occur until after the death of the deceased. This has no effect on the entitlement of others to legal rights, since the rights of the renouncing beneficiary are vested in that beneficiary at the point of the deceased's death (*Fisher v Dixon* (1840) 2 D 1121). If the widow in the example above does not renounce her claim to *jus relictae* until after her husband's death, the legitim fund will remain as one-third of the moveable estate notwithstanding the renunciation. Similarly, if a child renounces their entitlement to legitim after the death of their parent, their share of the fund is not redistributed amongst their siblings. In other words, accretion (where a renounced share 'accresces' to the legitim fund) does not operate. The value of the renounced legal rights will instead be made available to satisfy legacies if the deceased was testate or will fall into the free estate if the deceased was intestate.

Legal rights are most commonly renounced where alternative provision has been made for the claimant in the deceased's will. In such a situation, the claimant must choose between their legal rights and their inheritance under the will. As Hiram explains, 'to claim both is a contradiction, since it would be simultaneously to accept and reject the same instrument', namely the will. The need to make an election between the two options is referred to as the doctrine of approbate (meaning 'approve') and reprobate (meaning 'reject'), a common law rule now placed on a statutory footing by section 13 of the 1964 Act.

A claimant in this situation must receive proper legal advice on the consequences of making an election, or else the election may not be valid, following *Dawson's Trs v Dawson* (1896) 23 R 1006. The advice will generally clarify which of the two options will result in the larger payment to the claimant, though it will not always be the case that a claimant will make their choice based purely on financial considerations. A provisional election may be made before full advice is received, in which case the claimant retains the right to revoke the election, as demonstrated in *Harvie's Executors* v *Harvie's Trustees* 1981 SLT (Notes) 126. There is no time limit before which the election needs to be made, unless another legal rights claimant has good reason to require the decision within a particular period (*Stewart* v *Bruce's Trustees* (1898) 25 R 965). Should a claimant accept their inheritance under the will, they are considered to have implicitly renounced their legal rights claim. In practice, an executor is likely to require the claimant to execute a formal document of renunciation of legal rights when distributing legacies under the will. This is not least because only an express renunciation will prohibit any claim which might otherwise arise should an estate subsequently fall into intestacy or partial intestacy (*Nasmith* v *Boyes* (1899) 1 F (HL) 79).

If a claim to legal rights is neither satisfied nor renounced, it will be extinguished through the law of prescription 20 years from the date of death, under section 7 and schedule 1, para 2(f) of the Prescription and Limitation (Scotland) Act 1973.

DEFEATING LEGAL RIGHTS

Although it is not possible to exclude legal rights claims in a will or by any other mechanism, it is possible for a person to arrange their affairs in such a way that a claim will not have any value. As noted above, property disposed of by way of a will substitute will not form part of the estate on death and therefore cannot be subject to legal rights claims. Similarly, legal rights are payable only from the moveable estate, so that if an estate is made up entirely of heritage, there is no property from which legal rights can be claimed. More drastically, a person might arrange to have no property at all in their patrimony on death. Although the latter two techniques would be effective in defeating legal rights, there are obviously significant practical challenges to arranging one's affairs in this way, not least the fact that a person will rarely know the date of their death in advance. A person determined to avoid legal rights claims does have one foolproof method at their disposal, however – they must simply remain unmarried and have no children!

Essential facts

- A surviving spouse and any surviving children of the deceased are entitled to claim legal rights over the moveable estate, whether the deceased has left a will or not.

- A spouse is entitled to a third of the moveable estate if the deceased is also survived by children, or half of the moveable estate if there are no children.

- Children are entitled to a third of the moveable estate shared equally between them if the deceased is also survived by a spouse, or half the moveable estate shared equally between them if there is no spouse.

- Grandchildren may claim legal rights in place of their predeceasing parent. This is known as representation.

- Where a parent during their lifetime gives a gift to one child, but not to any of that child's siblings, the law treats the gift as an advance payment from the child's inheritance. The gift will therefore be taken into account in calculating the value of legal rights claims under the doctrine of collation.

- Legal rights may be extinguished through satisfaction, renunciation or prescription.

Essential cases

Coats' Trustees v Coats 1914 SC 744: Archibald Coats died, leaving behind two sons and three daughters. Each of the children had received collatable advances from their father during his lifetime. Each of the children had also been provided for in his will. One daughter, Evelyn, elected to take legitim rather than her inheritance under the will. The question was whether Evelyn and/or her siblings required to collate in this situation. The court noted that the doctrine of collation was an equitable doctrine designed to preserve equality amongst siblings when the legitim fund was divided. In this case, since only one child was concerned with the distribution of the legitim fund, there was no place for collation to operate. All the advances were accordingly ignored in calculation of the legitim claim.

Dawson's Trs v Dawson (1896) 23 R 1006: Mrs Dawson elected to take her inheritance under her late husband's will rather than her entitlement to *jus relictae*, based on legal advice she had received as to the value of the two different claims. It subsequently became clear that the legal advice had been wrong. The widow wished to revoke her election. The court found that, since there had been an error, and since nothing had happened as a result of her election which could not be undone without too much difficulty, she was free to revoke her election and take her legal rights entitlement instead.

Harvie's Executors v Harvie's Trustees (1981) SLT (Notes) 126: Mrs Harvie had to choose between provision under her husband's will and her entitlement to legal rights. After advice from a lawyer, she continued to live on her husband's farm, which was considered to be a provisional election in favour of the will, since she would have had no right to the farm in *jus relictae*. While she awaited a statement from the accountant on which to base her final election, she died. The court was satisfied that her actions were enough to amount to an election. It also indicated that, since the election was not injurious to her pecuniary interests, the election was binding despite the fact she had not received full legal advice.

FURTHER READING

JC Gardener, *The Origin and Nature of the Legal Rights of Spouses and Children in the Scottish Law of Succession* (1928)

Hiram, *Succession*, chapter 3

D Reid, "From the cradle to the grave: politics, families and inheritance law" (2008) 12 Edin LR 391

D Reid, "Why is it so difficult to reform the law of intestate succession?" (2020) 24 Edin LR 111

KGC Reid, MJ de Waal, R Zimmermann (eds), *Comparative Succession Law Volume III: Mandatory Family Protection* (2020), chapters 22–25

5 INTESTATE SUCCESSION

Where a person dies without making a will or any other provision for what should happen to their property on death, they are described as intestate. The law sets out a series of rules as to how an intestate estate should be distributed, contained primarily in the Succession (Scotland) Act 1964. The rationale underlying the rules is that they should, in so far as possible, achieve what it is thought deceased persons would have wanted. Although reform to this area of the law has been much debated in recent years, it remains unclear if or when any changes will take place. The potential for reform is discussed further in Chapter 11.

WHEN IS A PERSON INTESTATE?

Under section 36(1) of the 1964 Act, a person is intestate when they die leaving all or any part of their estate 'undisposed of by testamentary disposition'. The most common example of a testamentary disposition is a will, though other examples will be discussed in Chapter 6.

The deceased may have left a will covering only some of their property. In this case, the rules of intestate succession will be applied to the remainder of the estate. This is known as partial intestacy.

ORDER OF DISTRIBUTION

An intestate estate must be distributed in the following order:

(1) Payment of any debts owed by the deceased;
(2) Satisfaction from relevant assets of any prior rights claim (explained below) by a surviving spouse;
(3) Satisfaction from the remaining moveable estate of any legal rights claim (explained in Chapter 4) by a surviving spouse or child of the deceased;

(4)   Distribution of the free estate in line with the rules set out in statute (explained below).

If the deceased was in a cohabiting relationship on death, the surviving cohabitant is entitled to make a claim on the estate under section 29 of the Family Law (Scotland) Act 2006, explained below. A claim by a cohabitant must be paid after satisfaction of any prior rights or legal rights due to a surviving spouse, but *before* payment of legitim. In other words, the claim of a spouse will be prioritised over that of a cohabitant where the deceased had both. However, the cohabitant's claim will be prioritised over that of any children.

PRIOR RIGHTS

The law on prior rights is set out in sections 8 and 9 of the 1964 Act. In general terms, these provisions aim at ensuring a surviving spouse continues to have a home and some financial stability following the death of their partner.

Prior rights are available only to a surviving spouse, not to a cohabitant or children. They can be claimed from an intestate estate in addition to the spouse's legal rights. Prior rights are composed of three main entitlements: to a dwelling house; to furnishings for that house; and to a lump sum of money. These claims can be satisfied only where the estate includes sufficient, relevant assets. For example, if the deceased did not own a dwelling house on death, it is not possible for the spouse's claim in that regard to be satisfied. Each of the claims can be made independently of the others, however.

Legislation limits the value of assets which can be claimed in satisfaction of prior rights, with the values altered periodically to take account of inflation and other economic changes. The current limits, which will be discussed below, were set by the Prior Rights of Surviving Spouse and Civil Partner (Scotland) Order 2011 (SSI 2011/436) and have been in force since 1 February 2012.

The housing right

The first entitlement of the surviving spouse is to the interest of the deceased in a dwelling house. Where the family home was owned by the deceased, this will normally enable the spouse to inherit it or, where the home was commonly owned by the deceased and the spouse, to inherit the deceased's share of ownership.

'Dwelling house' is defined in section 8(6) of the 1964 Act. The definition is very wide, including houses and flats along with more uncommon types of dwelling such as caravans and houseboats. A garden or other ground attached to the dwelling is also included.

Section 8(1) provides that the entitlement will arise where the deceased had a 'relevant interest' in the dwelling, usually meaning ownership or a share of ownership. A tenant's interest in a dwelling will also be 'relevant', although succession to a tenancy will generally be further regulated by the legislation governing the form of tenancy in question.

Under section 8(4), a claim can be made to the deceased's interest in a dwelling only if the surviving spouse was 'ordinarily resident' there at the time of the deceased's death. What is meant by 'ordinarily resident' will depend on the dwelling. Ordinary residence in a holiday home in the countryside might only entail visiting every few weekends, for example. However, a dwelling in the deceased's estate in which the spouse has never resided – for example, a flat bought as an investment and rented out to others – will not be available as part of a prior rights claim.

Where the deceased had a relevant interest in more than one dwelling in which the surviving spouse was ordinarily resident, the spouse must elect which of the properties to take in satisfaction of their claim. Provision to this effect is made in section 8(1), which states that an election must be made within six months of the date of death.

The entitlement of the surviving spouse under this claim is capped at a value of £473,000. This does not entitle the spouse to claim interests in more than one dwelling, even if the combined value of those interests is below the cap. This may be explained by the legislation aiming to ensure the spouse has a home, rather than aiming to allow them to maximise their claim on the estate. Accordingly, only one interest in a dwelling can be claimed.

If the deceased's relevant interest in a dwelling is valued in excess of the statutory limit, the spouse will instead be entitled to a capital sum payment of £473,000. (In practice, the spouse will often negotiate with the executor to pay them the amount by which the statutory limit is exceeded and receive the interest in the dwelling in return.) The spouse may also receive a capital sum if the dwelling had been used by the deceased 'for carrying on a trade, profession or occupation', and the value of the estate as a whole is likely to be diminished by separating the house from the business. This might arise, for example, if the dwelling is a farmhouse but the spouse will not inherit the farm business, since the business may not be viable if the house is not part of its assets.

The furniture right

As a complement to the housing right, the surviving spouse is entitled to 'furniture and plenishings' under section 8(3) of the 1964 Act. 'Furniture and plenishings' are defined by section 8(6)(b) to cover most common household items including domestic animals, but excluding cash and securities along with any goods used for business purposes. Heirlooms are also excluded. The current financial limit on this entitlement is £29,000.

The spouse is entitled only to furniture from a dwelling in which they were ordinarily resident prior to the deceased's death. As with the claim to a dwelling itself, where the spouse was ordinarily resident in more than one home, section 8(1) provides that they must elect from which home they wish to inherit the furniture within six months of the date of death. Common sense suggests the spouse will usually elect the same home in respect of both dwelling and furniture claims, though it does not seem they are obliged to do so. It is also worth noting that section 25 of the Family Law (Scotland) Act 1985 sets out a presumption that ownership of household goods in the family home is shared between spouses. Accordingly, when valuing the prior rights claim of a spouse to furniture from the family home, it should be kept in mind that only a half share of ownership of these items presumptively forms part of the intestate estate, with the other half already in the spouse's patrimony.

The money right

The final prior rights entitlement of the surviving spouse, set out in section 9 of the 1964 Act, is to a sum of money. The spouse may claim up to £50,000 if the deceased is survived by children or further descendants, or up to £89,000 if there are no descendants.

The legislation specifies that this claim should be satisfied 'out of the parts of the intestate estate consisting of heritable and moveable property respectively in proportion to the respective amounts of those parts'. This means that the percentage of the money to be paid from the heritable property should be equivalent to the percentage of the remaining estate which is made up of heritable property. Similarly, the percentage of the money to be paid from the moveable property should be equivalent to the percentage of the remaining estate which is made up of moveable property.

This is best illustrated with an example. Assume that after the housing and furniture rights have been satisfied, there is £200,000 remaining in an intestate estate. £150,000, or 75% of the estate, is made up of heritage. £50,000, or 25% of the estate, is made up of moveables. The deceased has been survived by both a spouse and children, so the spouse is entitled to £50,000 in satisfaction of the money right. Seventy-five per cent of the remaining estate is made up of heritage, so 75% of the £50,000 claimed, which works out as £37,500, should be paid from the heritage. Twenty-five per cent of the remaining estate is made up of moveables, so 25% of the £50,000 claimed, or £12,500, should be paid from the moveables. The surviving spouse will accordingly receive £37,500 from the heritage and £12,500 from the moveables. Added together, this amounts to the £50,000 to which the spouse is entitled in terms of the money right.

The spouse's entitlement to a sum of money arises only once the housing right and the furniture right have been satisfied, or where those claims are excluded because there is no relevant property in the estate. Satisfaction of these earlier claims may mean that the total assets remaining in the estate are worth less than the capital sum to which the spouse is entitled. In that case, the claim will be satisfied by transfer to the surviving spouse of the entire remaining estate.

In a partially intestate estate, section 9(6)(b) provides that the value of any legacy to the surviving spouse under a testamentary deed must be offset against the money right, reducing the amount to which the spouse is entitled. This provision is given a wide meaning by section 36(1), so that a share in property received by the spouse by virtue of a survivorship destination or the proceeds of a life insurance policy will be offset against the prior rights claim to a capital sum. However, any legacy to which the spouse would otherwise have been entitled in satisfaction of their prior rights claim to a dwelling or furniture need not be offset against the money right.

An example may make the application of these provisions clearer. Kevin dies intestate. His estate comprises a half share in the family home worth £150,000, and savings of £25,000. His share in the home is subject to a survivorship destination in favour of his civil partner, Luke. Luke will receive Kevin's share in the house by virtue of the survivorship destination. If the survivorship destination had not existed, Luke would have received the half share in the house anyway by virtue of his prior rights claim to a dwelling. Accordingly, it is not necessary for Luke to offset the value of the share in the house against the capital sum to which he is entitled under prior rights. Luke will inherit Kevin's whole estate, with Kevin's half share in the family home transferred to Luke by way of the survivorship destination, and Kevin's savings of £25,000 transferred to Luke in satisfaction of the money right. Luke's prior rights claims to a dwelling and furniture will simply fall away, as the estate contains no assets from which these claims can be satisfied.

Where a spouse is entitled to a legacy in the will which *would* have to be offset against the money right, they may elect to renounce the legacy and claim the money right in full.

LEGAL RIGHTS

Following satisfaction of any prior rights claims, moveable property remaining in the estate is subject to legal rights claims by the surviving spouse and any issue of the deceased. Legal rights are explained in Chapter 4.

INTESTATE SUCCESSION

Following satisfaction of any legal rights claims, all property remaining in the estate, whether heritable or moveable, is referred to as the 'free estate'. It is also sometimes known as 'the dead's part' in recognition of the fact that this is the only part of the estate over which a deceased would have had full freedom to make provision in their will. The 1964 Act, somewhat confusingly, refers to the free estate as 'the intestate estate'. In order to avoid confusion, that terminology will not be used here.

The free estate is distributed to relatives of the deceased based on a hierarchy set out in section 2. The closest surviving relative or relatives of the deceased in terms of this hierarchy are referred to as the deceased's next-of-kin. Where there are any surviving relatives in the top tier of the hierarchy, the entire free estate will be shared amongst them. If there are no survivors in this tier, inheritance will fall to relatives in the second tier, and so on. As with legal rights, the doctrine of representation operates to enable children to share the entitlement of their predeceasing parent within each of the tiers.

At the top of the hierarchy of relatives are descendants of the deceased. Surviving children will share the entire free estate on a *per capita* basis. If a child has died before the deceased leaving behind grandchildren, the estate will be divided on a *per stirpes* basis. (For an explanation of the meaning of '*per capita*' and '*per stirpes*', see Chapter 4.) As discussed in Chapter 1, the definition of children includes posthumous children and adopted children, but not step-children of the deceased.

If there are no surviving descendants, inheritance will pass to the next tier of relatives, described as parents and 'collaterals' (siblings). This category includes adoptive parents and siblings. Where the deceased is survived by both parents and siblings, half the free estate will pass to their parent or parents, and half the free estate to their sibling or siblings, with each half shared equally between relevant survivors where there is more than one. For example, if the deceased is survived by a parent and two sisters, half the free estate will pass to the parent, and the other half to the sisters to share equally between them. If the deceased is survived only by a parent (or parents), or only by a sibling (or siblings), they receive the entire free estate, again to be shared equally where there is more than one. Representation operates in respect of siblings, with division of the estate on a *per stirpes* basis where a predeceasing sibling is survived by issue. For example, where the deceased is survived by a parent, a brother and the two children of a predeceasing sister, half the free estate will pass to the parent, a quarter to the brother, and the remaining quarter, which would have passed to the sister, is instead shared by the sister's two children. Half-blood siblings are entitled to inherit only if no full-blood siblings of the deceased survive. Neither step-parents nor step-siblings are entitled to inherit.

If the deceased is not survived by descendants, parents or siblings (including nieces and nephews), the inheritance will fall to a surviving spouse. It should be noted that the position of a surviving spouse in the hierarchy is likely to change soon. Section 77 of the Trusts and Succession (Scotland) Act 2024, due to be brought into force in April 2024, will amend section 2 of the 1964 Act to place a surviving spouse ahead of surviving parents and collaterals in the inheritance hierarchy. The result will be that where the deceased is survived by a spouse but no children, the spouse will take the whole estate (just as, under current law, the children take the whole estate when the deceased is survived by children but no spouse). Parents and collaterals will then form the third tier of the hierarchy, taking the free estate only where the deceased is survived by neither a spouse nor children.

The hierarchy then goes on to include more distant relatives: aunts and uncles, grandparents, siblings of grandparents and more remote relations. Finally, if no surviving relative can be found, section 7 of the 1964 Act provides that the Crown is entitled to the free estate as *ultimus haeres* (the 'final heir'). This function is exercised on behalf of the Crown by the King's and Lord Treasurer's Remembrancer, who will accept applications for claims on the estate from persons who may be considered to have a moral right to inherit.

COHABITANTS

Following the introduction of the Family Law (Scotland) Act 2006, a person who lived in a cohabiting relationship with the deceased at the time of death may make a claim on the intestate estate. Cohabitant is defined in section 25 of the Act as either member of a couple who were living together as if spouses or civil partners. To determine whether this definition has been met in a particular case, the court is directed to consider the length of time during which the parties lived together, the nature of their relationship during that period and the nature of any financial arrangements between them during that period. In the Scottish Law Commission's Report on Breakdown of Cohabitation (2022), it suggested the definition of cohabitant should be revised to focus on couples living together in 'an enduring family relationship', determined with reference to factors including the duration of the relationship, the extent to which the couple lived in the same residence, the extent to which they were financially interdependent and whether there were any children of the family. It is not yet clear whether the law will be amended in this respect, or if the amendments will apply in respect of succession claims by cohabitants in addition to the claims on the breakdown of a relationship which formed the focus of the SLC's recommendations.

The right of a cohabitant to claim on intestacy is set out at section 29(1). The court is empowered to make an order for a capital sum or a transfer of property to the surviving cohabitant after consideration of the factors listed in section 29(3). These are the size and nature of the net intestate estate, any benefit received or to be received by the survivor in consequence of the deceased's death from somewhere other than the intestate estate (for example, death in service benefit or the proceeds of a life insurance policy), the nature and extent of any other rights against or claims on the deceased's net intestate estate and any other matter the court considers appropriate. The only specific guidance the court is given as to the level of any award is that it must not exceed what a surviving spouse is or would have been entitled to receive under the 1964 Act regime, which takes into account prior rights, legal rights and any claim on the free estate if there are no children as explained above. As noted there, the surviving spouse will be placed at the head of the hierarchy for inheritance of the free estate if there are no children once the Trusts and Succession (Scotland) Act 2024 is brought into force. The amount they are entitled to receive under the 1964 Act – and by extension, the amount a surviving cohabitant is entitled to receive under the 2006 Act – may therefore increase, and by a significant margin in a large estate.

From the wording of the legislation, it is difficult to ascertain what a cohabitant might expect to receive from an application under section 29. The award is not directed towards any particular aim, such as ensuring the financial stability of the cohabitant or providing them with what the deceased would have wanted them to receive. In the second case decided under these provisions, *Windram, Applicant* 2009 Fam LR 157, Sheriff Janys M Scott QC indicated that it was unclear whether fairness in this context implied placing the cohabitant in the position a surviving spouse would have been in or protecting the rights of surviving children to what they would have been entitled to under the 1964 Act regime had there been no claim by a cohabitant.

The case law to date provides limited guidance. In *Savage v Purches* 2009 Fam LR 6, the sheriff was satisfied that the surviving cohabitant had lived with the deceased as if they were civil partners but did not believe any award to be justified. In part, this was because the applicant was already in receipt of a substantial sum (relative to the size of the estate) as the proceeds of life insurance. Additionally the deceased had not made a will specifying the applicant as a beneficiary, although evidence demonstrated that the deceased *had* done so in respect of an earlier long-term cohabiting partner. (That will had been destroyed when the earlier relationship came to an end.) In *Windram, Applicant*, the applicant was found to have been living with the deceased as if married for over 20 years, during which the couple had raised two children and operated a successful fish and chip shop business together. With the aim of striking a balance between the rights of the applicant and those of the children, the sheriff awarded the applicant £11,000 less than she would have been entitled to as a surviving spouse, enough to repay the outstanding loan on the family home which was held entirely in the name of the deceased.

The Scottish Government have recognised that reform to the legislation is likely to be necessary to clarify the intention behind this provision. If or when any reform will take place is unclear at present. This is discussed further in Chapter 11, along with consideration of potential reforms to the law of intestate succession more generally.

Essential facts

- An estate is intestate where the deceased did not leave a will.

- Where an estate is intestate, prior rights are paid first, followed by legal rights. A claim by a cohabitant will be paid after a spouse's legal rights but before legitim. Anything remaining once these claims are satisfied is known as free estate.

- Prior rights can be claimed by a surviving spouse and comprise a share in a house (up to a value of £473,000), furniture (up to a value of £29,000) and a lump sum of money (£50,000 if the deceased is survived by children, £89,000 if not) to be taken 'rateably' (proportionately) from the heritage and moveables in the estate.

- Legal rights of the spouse and/or children, as discussed in Chapter 4, are then paid from the remaining moveable estate.

- Finally, any free estate remaining is distributed to the deceased's nearest relative(s) as determined by the hierarchy set out in the 1964 Act, section 2.

- A surviving cohabitant of the deceased may make a claim under section 29 of the Family Law (Scotland) Act 2006. At present, there is little guidance on how much a cohabitant might expect to receive.

Essential cases

Savage v Purches 2009 Fam LR 6: Graham Voysey died leaving no will. Savage was his cohabiting partner and made a claim on his estate under section 29 of the 2006 Act. The defender was the deceased's half-sister, who stood to inherit the whole estate under the law of intestacy. In determining the claim, the court was satisfied that the pursuer and the deceased had 'lived together' in the meaning of the Act but did not make an award to the pursuer. Savage had already received a sizeable inheritance, relative to the size of the estate, as the proceeds of a life insurance policy in respect of the deceased. Additionally, Savage and Voysey did not have a shared bank account and Voysey had not made a will naming Savage as a beneficiary, all of which suggested to the court that the deceased would have intended Ms Purches to inherit rather than Mr Savage.

Windram, Applicant 2009 Fam LR 157: William Giopazzi died leaving no will. Windram was his cohabiting partner, and made a claim on his estate under section 29 of the 2006 Act. The action was defender by a *curator ad litem* representing the interests of the couple's children, who stood to inherit the whole estate under the law of intestacy. The court was satisfied that the couple had 'lived together' in the meaning of the Act for around 25 years. They had raised two children and ran a business together, although all assets were in the deceased's name. The court accepted that Ms Windram was essentially in the same position as a spouse, and made an award close to what a surviving spouse would have received on intestacy, with a small deduction to take account of an additional sum Ms Windram had received under an insurance policy. The court hoped this approach would balance the rights of Ms Windram with those of the children.

FURTHER READING

F Burns, "Surviving spouses, surviving children and the reform of total intestacy law in England and Scotland: past, present and future" (2013) 33(1) Legal Studies 85

Hiram, *Succession*, chapter 4

J Kerrigan, "Section 29 of the Family Law (Scotland) Act 2006 – the case for reform?" (2008) SLT 175

J Kerrigan, "Testamentary freedom revisited – further erosion?" (2012) SLT 29

Macdonald, *Succession*, chapter 4

F McCarthy, "Rights in succession for cohabitants: *Savage v Purches*" (2009) 13(2) Edin LR 325

MC Meston, *The Succession (Scotland) Act 1964* (5th ed, 2002) chapters 4 and 6

K Norrie, "Reforming Succession Law: Intestate Succession" (2008) 12(1)
    Edin LR 77
KGC Reid, MJ de Waal, R Zimmermann (eds), *Comparative Succession Law
    Volume II: Intestate Succession* (2015) chapter 19

EXAMPLE INTESTACY CALCULATION

In this example, the rules on legal rights and intestacy outlined in
Chapters 4 and 5 are used to demonstrate how an intestate estate
would be distributed amongst the various claimants.

Jay dies in an accident. He has not left a will. He leaves behind a
wife, Gloria, two sons, Mitchell and Manny, and two granddaughters,
Haley and Alex. The grandchildren are the kids of his daughter, Claire,
who died last year.

On death, Jay's estate comprises:

- A one-half share in the family home, which he had bought
  together with Gloria. The house is worth £450,000 in total.
- Furniture worth £20,000. This includes an antique table and
  chairs passed down to Jay by his grandfather, worth £5,000.
- A holiday cottage on Skye worth £50,000.
- Furniture for the holiday cottage worth £7,500.
- Investments worth £25,000.
- His stamp collection, valued at £10,000.
- A motorbike worth £12,500.
- Savings of £40,000.

	Heritable	*Moveable*	*Total estate*
House share	225,000		225,000
Furniture		15,000	15,000
Antiques		5,000	5,000
Holiday cottage	50,000		50,000
Cottage furniture		7,500	7,500
Investments		25,000	25,000
Stamp collection		10,000	10,000
Motorbike		12,500	12,500
Savings		40,000	40,000
TOTAL	**275,000**	**115,000**	**390,000**

	Heritable	Moveable	Total estate
Prior rights			
S8(1): housing[1]	225,000		
S8(3): furniture[2]		15,000	
	50,000	100,000	150,000
S9: money[3]			
Heritage: $50 \times \dfrac{50}{150}$	16,666		
Moveables: $50 \times \dfrac{100}{150}$		33,334	
Subtotal	**33,334**	**66,666**	**100,000**
Legal rights[4]			
Jus relictae: (66,666/3)		22,222	
Legitim: (66,666/3)		22,222[5]	
Intestate estate	**33,334**	**22,222**	**55,556**
Mitchell			18,518.66
Manny			18,518.66
(Claire)[6]			18,518.66

[1] Gloria will have to elect which of the two houses to receive, assuming she was ordinarily resident in both prior to Jay's death. It is assumed she will elect the more valuable family home. She is entitled to a share in a house up to a value of £473,000.

[2] Again, Gloria will have to elect which furniture she wishes to take. It is again assumed she will take the most valuable. The antique table and chairs will be excluded from the definition of furniture by section 8(3) of the Succession (Scotland) Act 1964. Gloria is entitled to furniture up to a value of £29,000.

[3] Jay is survived by descendants as well as a spouse: accordingly, Gloria is entitled to claim £50,000.

[4] As Jay is survived by descendants as well as a spouse, Gloria is entitled to one-third of the remaining moveables as *jus relictae*. The descendants will be entitled to one-third of the remaining moveables as legitim to be shared equally between them on a *per stirpes* basis.

[5] This amount, known as the legitim fund, will be split between Jay's surviving descendants on a *per stirpes* basis, with Mitchell and Manny receiving one-third, and Haley and Alex as Claire's representatives splitting the final third of the legitim fund between them.

[6] Since Claire predeceased her father, her share will be split between her two children, Haley and Alex, who will therefore receive £6,172.88 each.

Division of the legitim fund

Total fund: £22,222

Children (two surviving, one predeceased leaving descendants): 3

Each child receives: £22,222/3 = £7,407.33

Claire's share will be split between her two children, so Haley and Alex will receive £3,703.66 each.

Summary of division of estate

Gloria

Housing right	225,000
Furniture	15,000
S9 money	50,000
Jus relictae	22,222
TOTAL	**312,222**

Mitchell and Manny

Legitim	7,407.33
Free estate	18,518.66
TOTAL	**25,925.99 (each)**

Haley and Alex

Legitim	3,703.66
Free estate	9,259.33
TOTAL	**12,962.99 (each)**

Final summary

Gloria	312, 222
Mitchell	25,925.99
Manny	25,925.99
Haley	12,962.99
Alex	12,962.99
TOTAL	**389,999.96**

6 MAKING A WILL

This chapter considers the creation, revocation and rectification of testamentary writings. A testamentary writing or 'testament' is a deed, such as a will, setting out what the granter wishes to happen to their property when they die. A testament will be valid where the granter had capacity to 'test' (to make a will) which was exercised freely (referred to as **essential validity**), and where the deed meets the statutory requirements for legal writing set out in the Requirements of Writing (Scotland) Act 1995 (referred to as **formal validity**). Public policy places some **restraints on testamentary freedom**, and provisions in an otherwise valid testament which exceed these restraints will be invalid. A valid testament may be **revoked** by the granter while still alive or may be deemed to have been revoked where certain conditions are met. A testament which is valid but does not accurately reflect the granter's wishes may be **rectified** by the court after the granter's death in certain circumstances.

The most common form of testamentary writing is a will. A will may be one single document, but wills can also be made up of several documents, perhaps written and executed at different times. An addition to a will is known as a codicil. In general, a will operates to transmit the deceased's property into the hands of an executor, who then transfers it to the beneficiaries named in the will. A trust disposition and settlement is a more complex form of testamentary writing, transferring property on the testator's death into the hands of trustees who will administer property on behalf of the beneficiaries named in the deed.

MAKING A WILL: ESSENTIAL VALIDITY

The first requirement for validity of a testament is that the granter formed a completed testamentary intention. There are three aspects to this. Firstly, the testator must have reached the minimum age at which legal capacity to test is recognised and have been mentally capable of making a will. Secondly, the testator must have exercised their intention to test freely and not been overcome by pressure from another person through facility and circumvention or undue influence. Finally, the deed must represent the granter's completed intention, not simply thoughts on what they may or may not wish to happen in future.

Capacity

In Scotland, a person has testamentary capacity from the age of 12 onwards under section 2(2) of the Age of Legal Capacity (Scotland) Act 1991. A person who has reached that age must also have the necessary mental capacity to understand the nature and consequences of their testament at the time it is granted. Authorities such as *Sivewright* v *Sivewright's Trustees* 1920 SC (HL) 63 have given approval in Scots law to the classic English formulation of this requirement, set out in *Banks* v *Goodfellow* (1869–70) LR 5 QB 549:

> It is essential to the exercise of [the power to test] that a testator shall understand the nature of the act and its effects; shall understand the extent of the property of which he is disposing; shall be able to comprehend and appreciate the claims to which he ought to give effect; and, with a view to the latter object, that no disorder of the mind shall poison his affections, pervert his sense of right, and prevent the exercise of his natural faculties – that no insane delusion shall influence his will in disposing of his property and bring about a disposal of it which if the mind had been sound would not have been made.

Shortly put, the testator must understand the consequences of their actions in writing the deed. It is not necessary that the intentions contained in the deed should be objectively fair or morally justifiable, only that the testament was made in full understanding of the results. For example, in *Morrison* v *MacLean's Trustees* (1862) 24 D 625, the deceased left part of his estate for the benefit of his housekeeper, and the rest in trust for the education of boys named MacLean. No provision was made for any surviving family members. The court did not consider this in itself evidence of a lack of capacity on the testator's part.

Capacity may not be a permanent state, but may come and go where a person is affected by a condition such as dementia. What matters is that the testator had the relevant capacity at the time when the testament was executed. In *Nisbet's Trustees* v *Nisbet* (1871) 9 M 937, it was held that where the deceased was known to have suffered from a condition which impaired their capacity, a person seeking to rely on the will must prove that it was executed at a time when the testator was lucid. This is a reversal of the normal situation. It seems that if the terms of the will itself are irrational – for example, if the estate was left to the Man on the Moon – then the testator is likely to be found to lack capacity.

The testator may also have lacked capacity temporarily where under the influence of alcohol or drugs. The English decision of *Sharp* v *Adam* [2006] EWCA Civ 449 concerned a testator who had been suffering from multiple sclerosis. Evidence suggested that his mood was altered by the drug therapy he was receiving at the time of executing his will to such an extent that he was not rational. The will he had made at this time, which excluded his daughters entirely, was held to be invalid, and a previous will leaving everything to them was accordingly revived.

Facility and circumvention

A testament executed by a testator with relevant capacity may nevertheless be challenged if that capacity was not exercised freely. A testament may be reduced if it resulted from the illegitimate influence of a third party over the granter. In other words, if a will was written as a result of the granter being placed under pressure of certain types, it may not stand.

Challenges of this type are most frequently based on the doctrine of facility and circumvention or the doctrine of undue influence. In practice, a testament may be subject to challenges under both doctrines since it is difficult to draw a clear boundary line between the two. Lord President Clyde gave a summary in *Ross* v *Gosselin's Exrs* 1926 SC 325:

> The essence of undue influence is that a person, who has assumed or undertaken a position of quasi-fiduciary responsibility in

relation to the affairs of another, allows his own self-interest to deflect the advice or guidance he gives, in his own favour. On the other hand, the essence of circumvention and facility is that a person practises on the debility of another whose individuality is impaired by infirmity or age, and moulds the inclination of the latter to his own profit.

It is quite possible for both facility and circumvention and undue influence to have been present in the same case.

Facility and circumvention is established where three elements are present – facility, circumvention and lesion. The starting point will be lesion, meaning loss. This can be understood as loss suffered by the testator where their will did not express their freely formed intention, or loss suffered by a person who would have inherited if the will had reflected the testator's true intention, known as a disappointed beneficiary. Practically speaking, without a disappointed beneficiary, no-one is likely to have an interest in challenging the will after the testator's death.

Facility is defined by Hiram (para 6.8) as 'weakness of mind such that the mind of the person affected is easily swayed by that of another'. Although the case law does not set out a clear test, the key concept is that the testator must have been more susceptible to influence, or less able to resist suggestion, than the average person. The level of suggestibility cannot be such that the testator lacks capacity entirely, however. Facility may result from circumstances such as senility, mental illness or the influence of intoxicants. However, it will not automatically follow that the testator was in a state of facility solely because one of these elements was present. It will be a question of fact in every case.

Circumvention is defined in *Bell's Dictionary* as 'deceit or fraud', and described by Hiram (para 6.09) as 'pressure of some kind exerted on the testator by a third party'. This element will often be difficult to evidence: the actions of a third party amounting to circumvention are unlikely to have been witnessed by anyone other than the testator, and by the time a challenge is brought, the testator is most likely to be dead. The court has been willing to infer the existence of circumvention where the degree of facility is high, loss is established and there is evidence of factual circumstances in which circumvention could have taken place.

The lead case of *MacGilvary* v *Gilmartin* 1986 SLT 89 provides an example. In the weeks immediately following the death of the pursuer's husband, the defender – who was the pursuer's daughter – took the pursuer to a solicitor and had the pursuer sign deeds transferring ownership of her house to the defender. Afterwards, the pursuer argued that she had been in a state of extreme grief at the time such as to amount to facility, and had not known what she was signing. There was no specific evidence of circumvention on the defender's part. The court found that the degree of facility and the level of lesion, together with the absence of any reasonable explanation of the defender's behaviour, were sufficient to give rise to an inference of circumvention from the facts. The disposition transferring ownership of the house was accordingly set aside. More recently, in *Horne* v *Whyte* [2005] CSOH 115, the testator had been heavily dependent on his housekeeper who had latterly looked after his legal affairs as well as his house and his health. Late in life, he made a codicil to his will reducing the legacies to his family members in order to leave a substantial sum to the housekeeper. The court found that only circumvention on her part could have caused the amendments to the will.

Undue influence

Undue influence is established where three elements are present – a relationship of trust between the testator and another party, an abuse of that trust by the other party and an advantage obtained by the other party as a result. The testator does not need to be in a state of facility for a challenge of this type to be successful, and may be in robust mental health. In this case, it is the testator's trust in the other party that makes it possible for advantage to be taken.

A relationship of trust is likely to exist between the testator and a party with whom they are close personally or professionally. Such a relationship will be presumed between near relatives, as with the mother and son in *Gray* v *Binny* (1879) 7 R 332. The relationship between a solicitor and a client was found to meet the test in *Ross* v *Gosselin's Exrs* 1926 SC 325. The relationship between the testator and her art dealer in *Honeyman's Exrs* v *Sharp* 1978 SC 223 also satisfied the test, although the evidence made clear that the art dealer had become close with the testator and was advising her on business affairs more generally by the time the will under challenge was executed. Relationships which fall within this category will usually be fiduciary or quasi-fiduciary, and their existence in each case will be determined as a matter of fact.

Evidence must also be brought of how that trust has been abused. The other party may have misrepresented to the testator the effect the will would have, or have misrepresented the actions of persons such as the testator's family members to dissuade the testator from making provision for them in the will. It is important to demonstrate that the testator would not have listened to the other party, or taken heed of their actions, if it were not for the existing relationship of trust between the two. A testator is likely to ignore a stranger on the street who suggests the testator's child does not deserve to be included in the testator's will, but if this suggestion is made by a trusted adviser who claims to be concerned for the testator's interests, the outcome may be quite different.

Finally, the other party must have received a benefit as a result of exerting influence on the testator. This would usually take the form of a legacy in the will that the other party would not otherwise have received, or a more generous legacy than might have been expected.

Given the nature of the undue influence doctrine, it should not be surprising that it is difficult to mount a successful challenge on this ground where the testator has received independent legal advice in relation to the will. This point was emphasised in *Gray* v *Binny* (1879) 7 R 332.

Where facility and circumvention or undue influence are shown to have been present, the testament can be set aside (reduced). This may result in the revival of an earlier will, as discussed below. The existence of an earlier will more favourable to certain beneficiaries is likely to be the catalyst for a challenge on these grounds – the testator's children, say, to whom the entire estate had been left in an earlier will may be motivated to challenge a testament granted three days before death in which the deceased left everything to their housekeeper. Where a testament is successfully challenged, but no prior will exists, the estate will fall into intestacy and be distributed on that basis.

Completed testamentary intention

Where a testator has freely exercised their capacity to test, the deed must be clear that the granter intended it to have testamentary effect. Hiram (para 5.4) summarises: 'The decisive factor is whether or not it can be established that the testator meant the deed in question to represent his or her concluded testamentary intention'. In other words, the document must represent the testator's final word on the matter of where their assets are to go. A document indicating an intention to make a will at a later stage or sketching out some thoughts on what a person *might* wish to happen on their death will not meet this requirement. A letter to a solicitor instructing her to draft a will for the testator cannot represent a completed testamentary intention following *Munro* v *Coutts* (1813) 1 Dow 437.

MAKING A WILL: FORMAL VALIDITY

A testament which is essentially valid must also meet the requirements for formal legal writing. The sample will at the end of Chapter 7 of this book gives an example of how a formally valid testamentary writing could look in practice. (It should be noted that testaments executed prior to 1 August 1995 are subject to an older set of requirements for formal validity, details of which are given by Hiram (paras 5.5–5.12).)

The Requirements of Writing (Scotland) Act 1995 is the key piece of legislation in this area. The Act does not prescribe the use of a particular document template or necessitate the inclusion of specific words within a testament. Instead, it provides two general requirements for validity. First, the will must be in writing (section 1(2)(c)). A verbal statement cannot be a valid testament. Second, the deed must be subscribed by the granter, meaning the testator must sign at the end of the last page of the will (section 2). Section 7 of the Act sets out three forms of signature acceptable in this context: the longstop method, where the testator signs using the full form of their name as employed in the will, such as *James Andrew Smith*; the standard method, where the testator signs using a full or abbreviated version of his forename together with his surname, such as *Jim Smith*; or the informal method, where the testator signs using any other name, description, initial or mark, such as *JAS* or *Dad*.

Provided the will is written down and has been subscribed by the testator, it will be formally valid. If the will is to be implemented, however, formal validity will not be enough. The will must also be probative.

The term probative means 'self-proving'. This is relevant where a challenge is made to the validity of a will. As a general rule, a person who seeks to rely on a deed has responsibility to prove the validity of that deed if it is challenged. In the context of succession, this would mean a beneficiary who sought to rely on a will to claim a legacy would have to prove the validity of the will in court if any person claimed, for example, that the testator lacked capacity to make it. Where a will has been made probative, however, the responsibility changes sides. If a challenge is made to the validity of a probative will, the law presumes that the will *was* validly executed at the date and place narrated in the deed. The onus accordingly falls on the challenger to show that the execution was in some way defective.

In practice, it is often difficult to evidence the circumstances in which a testament was executed, because a challenge generally will not occur until after the testator's death, at which point the testator can no longer speak for themselves. Ensuring the will is probative, and therefore benefits from a presumption of validity, may be particularly important to a testator as reassurance that the intentions they express in the deed will not be thwarted. On a more practical note, only a probative will can form the basis of confirmation of an executor-nominate, as discussed in Chapter 3.

A testament can be made probative only where the testator has subscribed using either the longstop or standard methods of signature. Although a will subscribed using the informal method ('*Dad*') is valid, it is not possible for it to become probative.

Where a longstop or standard signature has been used, two further steps are necessary for probativity. First, section 3(2) of the 1995 Act provides that the will must be signed by the testator on every page. A signature anywhere on the page will suffice for every page except the final one, where subscription (a signature at the foot of the page) is required.

The second requirement for probativity, set out in section 3(1)(a) of the 1995 Act, is that the testator's subscription must have been witnessed. The witnessing or 'attestation' process is regulated by section 3. The witness must be 16 years of age or above, have full legal capacity and 'know' the granter in the sense of being certain of the granter's identity. The Act does not prohibit a beneficiary under the will acting as a witness, but as a matter of good practice, this is usually avoided. The testator must subscribe the will in the presence of the witness or else acknowledge to the witness that the subscription is the testator's signature. The witness then signs to confirm that the subscription is the testator's signature. This must be 'one continuous process', meaning the witness must sign immediately after watching the testator subscribe or having the testator acknowledge their signature. The name and address of the witness must be added to the document after the witness has signed. This is usually contained in the 'testing clause' which follows the end of the document. By signing, the witness confirms only that the subscription on the will is the testator's signature. The witness is not confirming the content of the will beyond that.

Whilst the testator remains alive, it is always possible to convert a valid will into a probative will by the testator acknowledging their signature to a witness. After the testator has died, this will obviously no longer be possible. However, the 1995 Act allows for the will to be declared probative by the court following an application by any interested party under section 4. An executor-nominate may make an application under this section when seeking confirmation.

Alterations made to a testament after it has been subscribed are not part of the deed, except where the alteration has also been signed by the testator. In practice the testator will usually initial any changes for this reason. Section 5 of the 1995 Act provides, however, that alterations will be presumed to have been made prior to subscription in certain circumstances, including where the will is probative. Accordingly, the onus in most cases will be on a person arguing that the alteration was made after subscription to prove that this was the case.

MAKING A WILL: RESTRAINTS ON TESTAMENTARY FREEDOM

Public policy considerations place certain limitations on the testator's power to dispose of their property on their death. The law will deem provisions of a will invalid where they are of no public or private benefit or where they attempt to exercise too much control from 'beyond the grave'.

Testamentary provisions focused on memorialising the testator after their death are the primary example of provisions which do not confer any benefit on a living individual or on the public in general. In the notorious case of *McCaig* v *University of Glasgow* 1907 SC 231, the testator had directed that the income from his estate should be used in perpetuity to build towers and statues of himself and his family on his land. His sister challenged this provision on the basis that it would disinherit his family without creating a benefit for anyone else. The court accepted that testamentary provision for a memorial or burial place of a normal scale would be valid, but directing the whole income of a large estate to works of 'no utility' was held to be invalid. Curiously, and notwithstanding her successful challenge in this case, the testator's sister went on to make similar provision in her own will, which was again held invalid by the court (*McCaig's Trustees* v *Kirk Session of United Free Church of Lismore* 1915 SC 426). A similar example can be found in *Aitken's Trustees* v *Aitken* 1927 SC 374, though in *Campbell Smith's Trustees* v *Scott* 1944 SLT 198, a large sum of money bequeathed to build a monument to the Royal Scots army regiment was held to be valid.

When drafting their testament, the testator may provide that a legacy should pass to a beneficiary only where certain conditions are satisfied, as discussed further in Chapter 7. If such conditions are illegal, immoral or impossible, the legacy will remain valid but the condition will be declared *pro non scripto* ('as if it had not been written'), meaning the legacy will be distributed as if the condition had not existed. A condition which purports to constrain the beneficiary's freedom to marry, for example by requiring that the beneficiary does or does not marry a particular person in order to receive the legacy, will be found *pro non scripto* on this basis (*Barker* v *Watson's Trustees* 1919 SC 109). Similarly, a condition on where or with whom a person can live is likely to be declared invalid as in *Fraser* v *Rose* (1849) 11 D 1466 and *Balfour's Trustees* v *Johnston* 1936 SC 137.

There are also limits on the extent to which a testator can control the destiny of their property after death. Historically in Scotland, heritage forming the ancestral seat of a wealthy family would be handed down from first son to first son in perpetuity through the use of a legal device called an entail (or tailzie) introduced by the Entail Act 1685. This device became essentially unusable as the result of a series of statutory restrictions placed on it during the 1800s, and the 1685 Act itself was eventually repealed by the Abolition of Feudal Tenure (Scotland) Act 2000. A testator may attempt to exert control over property after their death by instructing it to be placed in trust and directing the trustees on management of the property over a long period of time, but legislation limits the extent of the powers of a truster in this respect. This complex topic belongs to the law of trusts and will not be addressed further here.

REVOKING A WILL

A testator may revoke a will at any point during their lifetime provided they have capacity to do so. The capacity requirements outlined above in relation to creation of a will also apply to revocation of a will. A testator with capacity will be unable to revoke a will if they have contracted not to do so with a beneficiary. A contract of this kind is competent (*Paterson* v *Paterson* (1893) 20 R 484) but must be in writing (*McEleveen* v *McQuillan's Executrix* (1997) SLT (Sh Ct) 46).

A testator can revoke their will by destroying it. This may be straightforward physical destruction of the deed – burning it in the fire – or symbolic destruction, where the will is scribbled out as in *Cruickshank's Trustees* v *Glasgow Magistrates* (1887) 14 R 603, or cut into pieces as in *Crosbie* v *Wilson* (1865) 3 M 870.

Destruction will revoke a will only where the testator has intentionally destroyed their own deed, or instructed someone else to do so as in *Cullen's Exr* v *Elphinstone* 1948 SC 662. Where a will which is known to exist cannot be found after the testator's death, it is presumed the testator has intentionally destroyed it. Any person seeking to overturn this presumption must raise an action to 'prove the tenor' of the will. Success in an action of this kind requires sufficient evidence to prove the content of the will and also to prove that the will was not destroyed by the testator. Cases in which such evidence is available are not common.

A testator may also revoke a will through subsequent testamentary writing. A testator will usually do so expressly, by executing a new will which includes a 'revocation clause'. A clause of this kind provides that only the will containing the clause represents the granter's completed testamentary intention and that earlier writings are revoked. Subsequent testamentary writing without such a clause may nevertheless revoke an earlier will, or part of it, by implication. Where a will contains provisions which conflict with those in an earlier deed by the same granter, the earlier deed is presumed to be revoked to the extent that it conflicts with the later deed. Imagine, for example, that Olive executes a will in February leaving her house to Padma and her jewellery to Rose. In December of the same year, she executes a second will, providing nothing other than that she leaves her house to Simon. The legacy of the house to Padma in the February deed will be revoked by the conflicting legacy in favour of Simon in the December deed. However, the legacy of the jewellery to Rose in the February deed will stand, since it creates no conflict with anything in the December deed. If a later will disposes of the whole estate, the earlier deed must logically be revoked entirely, as in *Cadger* v *Ronald's Trustees* 1946 SLT (Notes) 24.

Where a testament is revoked by a subsequent deed, then that subsequent deed is itself revoked, does the original testament revive? The answer to this question was put beyond doubt by the Succession (Scotland) Act 2016. Section 5 of that Act provides that revocation of a subsequent deed will not revive an earlier will. A testator who wished to revive an earlier testament would have to execute a new deed doing so expressly.

Finally, a testament may be impliedly revoked through operation of the *conditio si testator sine liberis decesserit*. This *conditio* operates where the testator has had a child subsequent to execution of the will. The law presumes that a testator would not deliberately omit to make testamentary provision for the child. The effect of the *conditio* is to revoke all testamentary writings of the parent, rendering the estate intestate.

This does not happen automatically. Rather, the child born after the will was executed must decide whether they wish to invoke the *conditio*. The decision may not be straightforward. It should be recalled that a child is always entitled to legal rights from their parent's estate, as discussed in Chapter 4. Where the estate is testate, a legal rights claim must be satisfied before any legacies are distributed. Where the estate is intestate, however, a legal rights claim will be satisfied only after payment of prior rights claimed by a surviving spouse and payment of any claim made by a surviving cohabitant, as discussed in Chapter 5. In many cases, satisfaction of prior rights will exhaust the estate entirely, leaving nothing with which a legal rights claim can be paid. A child seeking to maximise their claim would therefore be advised to invoke the *conditio* only where the deceased has no surviving spouse or cohabitant, or where the estate is so large that assets greater than the value of a legitim claim will remain after the rights of a spouse or cohabitant have been satisfied.

The presumption that a testator would not intentionally omit to provide for a child born after the will was executed can be overturned where evidence shows the omission was deliberate. Clear evidence of a positive intention to exclude the child will be required. In *Stuart-Gordon* v *Stuart-Gordon* (1899) 1 F 1005, the testator had been in ill health and had executed her will around the time the child was born. Evidence showed that she knew the child would be well provided for by other sources. The court found that this combination of factors was sufficient to overturn the presumption, meaning the *conditio* could not be invoked. Evidence that significant time has passed since the birth without a new will being made will not rebut the presumption, as demonstrated by *Milligan's JF* v *Milligan* 1910 SC 58, in which ten years had passed between the child's birth and the testator's death.

RECTIFYING A WILL

Sections 3 and 4 of the Succession (Scotland) Act 2016 allow for rectification of a will by a court. Rectification is possible after the testator's death where the will was drafted not by the testator, but by a person or persons acting on the testator's instructions, such as a solicitor. If the court is satisfied that the will fails to accurately express what was instructed, the court may order rectification of the will in whatever way is necessary to reflect those instructions. The court is entitled to have regard to extrinsic evidence (in other words, evidence beyond the will itself) in determining whether rectification is necessary. An application for rectification must be made within six months of the testator's death, although the court may accept late applications where there is good cause.

Essential facts

- A will is valid where the testator freely exercised their capacity to form a completed testamentary intention and the deed meets the statutory formalities of writing.
- A testator has capacity if they have reached the age of 12 and are capable of understanding the effect of making a will.
- The testator's capacity may not have been freely exercised if they have been put under pressure by another person. A will can be challenged in cases of facility and circumvention (where a vulnerable testator is deceived or misled by another person) and undue influence (where a person takes advantage of the trust placed in them by the testator).
- The Requirements of Writing (Scotland) Act 1995 provides that a will must be in writing and subscribed on the final page by the testator.
- A will becomes probative (self-proving) when it is signed on every page and the testator's signature is witnessed by another person. Where a will is probative, any person challenging the validity of that will has the responsibility of proving it to be invalid.
- Provisions in a will which are contrary to public policy will be held invalid. Conditions on a legacy which are contrary to public policy will be deemed *pro non scripto*.
- A will may be revoked by a testator freely exercising their capacity to do so at any time in their life.

- A testator may revoke a will by intentionally destroying it.

- A testator may also revoke a will by subsequent testamentary writing which expressly revokes the earlier will or which contains provisions which conflict with those in the earlier will.

- A child born after a will was executed may invoke the *conditio si testator* to revoke the will if it does not provide for them.

- A will drafted for the testator by another person may be rectified by the court if necessary to accurately reflect the testator's instructions to that person.

Essential cases

MacGilvary v Gilmartin 1986 SLT 89: In the days immediately following her husband's death, Mrs McGilvary was taken to a solicitor by her daughter, Mrs Gilmartin, where she disponed the house to her daughter. Mrs MacGilvary later argued that she was in an extreme state of grief and did not know what she was doing at the time. She wished to have the disposition set aside on the basis of facility and circumvention. The court accepted that her grief was enough to demonstrate facility on the testator's part, and also that she had suffered a loss in signing over her house. Although there was no specific evidence of circumvention, the high degree of both facility and loss allowed the court to infer that circumvention must have been present, and the disposition was set aside.

Gray v Binny (1879) 7 R 332: The pursuer was in line to receive a substantial inheritance. The defender – the pursuer's mother – and her solicitor with whom she was close, convinced the defender to sign away his rights to the inheritance for far less than it was worth in order that the pursuer could pay off her debts. Evidence suggested that the defender was not familiar with the business world and placed complete trust in the pursuer. Undue influence was held to exist, since the defender had taken advantage of the trust placed in her by the pursuer to her own benefit.

FURTHER READING

J Chalmers, "Testamentary conditions and public policy" in KGC Reid, MJ de Waal and R Zimmermann (eds), *Exploring the Law of Succession* (2007)

Hiram, *Succession*, chapters 5, 6 and 10

Macdonald, *Succession*, chapters 6, 8 and 9

KGC Reid, MJ de Waal and R Zimmermann (eds), *Comparative Succession Law Volume I: Testamentary Formalities* (2011) chapter 18

7 TESTATE SUCCESSION

A testament is primarily composed of legacies, meaning provisions stating who is to receive the testator's property on their death. Where there is a valid will, distribution of the estate should therefore be a relatively straightforward matter of the executor complying with the terms of the will after paying any debts or legal rights claims. Difficulties can however arise where the provisions of the will are not clear or where they cannot be given effect. This chapter considers some of these difficulties and the legal rules which may help to resolve them.

The first part of the chapter considers problems connected to the **subject of a legacy**, meaning the property with which the legacy is concerned. The second part of the chapter looks at problems connected to the **object of a legacy**, meaning the person in whose favour the legacy has been granted, also known as the beneficiary or legatee. This section includes discussion of **destinations**, which are provisions on what should happen to property following the death of the legatee identified in the will. The **example will** included at the end of this chapter helps to illustrate some of the points discussed, and is referred to where relevant.

GENERAL PRINCIPLES

The broad aim of the court when interpreting a testament will be to give effect to the testator's wishes based on what is said in the deed. The court will therefore tend to favour an interpretation of particular words or clauses that avoids any part of the estate falling into intestacy.

When interpreting a will, it should be read as a whole document, with its meaning drawn solely from the words used. Reference to extrinsic evidence is excluded by section 8 of the Law Reform (Miscellaneous Provisions) (Scotland) Act 1985. Extrinsic evidence may, however, be permitted where it is impossible to determine the meaning of the words used without it. An example is the case of *Nasmyth's Trustees* v *National Society for the Prevention of Cruelty to Children* 1914 SC (HL) 76. The testator had left a legacy to 'the National Society for the Prevention of Cruelty to Children'. The legacy was claimed by both the London-based charity of that name and the equivalent Scottish organisation called the Scottish Society for the Prevention of Cruelty to Children. The Scottish charity was permitted to lead extrinsic evidence to suggest that the testator, who was Scottish and whose estate was held entirely in Scotland, was not aware of the existence of the London-based charity. However, the evidence was not sufficiently strong to displace the clear wording of the will, meaning that the London-based charity was found to be the intended legatee.

THE SUBJECT OF A LEGACY

The subject of a legacy is the property which it bequeaths. One important way in which the law categorises legacies is by reference to their subjects.

A **specific legacy** is a bequest of a particular piece of property, such as a house or an item of jewellery. The property may be singular or plural, so a bequest of a collection of books would be a specific legacy in the same way as a bequest of a first edition of *Pride and Prejudice*. If the subject of a specific legacy has been destroyed or disposed of by the testator during their lifetime, the legacy is not payable and the legatee has no right to anything else in its place. A specific legacy will fail if the subject is not described clearly enough to be identifiable. In the sample will at the end of this chapter, the legacy of the Fender Telecaster guitar is a specific legacy. The guitar is described in sufficient detail to distinguish it from other guitars which may form part of the testator's estate. The legacy of shares in Apple Records PLC is also specific.

A **demonstrative legacy** is a type of specific legacy, where the property bequeathed is to come from a specific named source. The most common example is a legacy of an amount of money to be paid from a particular bank account.

A **general legacy** is a bequest of generic property which cannot be distinguished from other property of the same class. The most common example is a legacy of an amount of money with no specification as to the source from which the money should be paid. In the sample will, the legacy of £300 is general.

The subject of a **residual legacy** is the residue of the estate, meaning everything left in the estate after debts, legal rights claims and other legacies have been paid. It is not uncommon for the residue to represent the entire estate or the bulk of the estate, after small legacies have been left to other beneficiaries as tokens. The residual legacy is at clause seven of the example will. Where a legacy in one of the other categories fails for any reason, the subject of that legacy will fall into the residue. Similarly, where a surviving spouse or child elects to take legal rights rather than the provision made for them in the will as discussed in Chapter 4, the subjects of the legacy or legacies from which they would have benefitted fall into the residue. If the residual legacy fails, the residue of the estate will become intestate and be distributed based on the rules of intestate succession discussed in Chapter 5.

Legacies may be **conditional**. The testator may impose a suspensive condition on the legacy, meaning that the legacy takes effect *only if* a certain condition is fulfilled. A common example would be provision by the testator that a beneficiary should take a legacy 'only if he survives me for fourteen days or more'. The testator may alternatively impose a resolutive condition on the legacy, meaning that the legacy takes effect *unless* a certain condition is fulfilled. For example, the testator may specify that a beneficiary should take a legacy 'unless he is no longer in full time education at the time of my death'. The law places certain restrictions on the content of conditions which may be validly imposed by a testator, discussed in Chapter 6.

Difficulties can arise in determining whether a direction in the will is a condition or a trust purpose. In *Dunbar* v *Scott's Trustees* (1872) 10 M 982, the testator had left £2,000 to A provided that the testator had not purchased A a commission in the army by the time of the testator's death. Was this a suspensive condition – that the money was to pass to A only if the testator had not purchased him a commission before death – or a trust purpose, to the effect that A was to inherit the money only for use in buying himself a commission? If the latter, the legacy would have failed for impossibility, since it was no longer possible to purchase commissions in the army by the time of the testator's death. The court construed the testator's words as imposing a condition on the legacy, allowing the money to be paid to A.

A legacy may be described as **precatory** if it does not represent a completed testamentary intention but is merely the testator's wish as to what might happen to the property in future. For a legacy to be precatory in its entirety is unusual. It is more common for a valid legacy to contain precatory elements. For example, in *Milne v Smith* 1982 SLT 129, the testator left shares in two businesses to his son 'it being my wish that both these businesses should be combined by my son and my brother'. The legacy of the shares was valid, but the testator could not compel his son to enter into a partnership with his brother. That aspect of the bequest was merely precatory.

Legacies will usually involve transfer of ownership from the deceased's estate to the legatee. However, it is possible for the testator to make periodical provision for the beneficiary through the alternative mechanisms of **annuity** and **liferent**.

An annuity is the right to an annual payment from a specified source for a specified period of time. For example, Terry may include provision in his will that Una is to receive an annuity of 25% of the income from Terry's premium bonds for ten years after Terry's death, or until she remarries.

A liferent is a right to the use and fruits of property for the duration of the holder's lifetime. Where the property in question is heritage, the legatee has a real right of liferent (sometimes referred to as 'proper liferent') which entitles the liferenter to occupy the house until death. Where the property in question is moveables, the legatee is the beneficiary under a lifetime trust (sometimes referred to as 'improper liferent') which entitles the beneficiary to receive income generated from investments throughout their lifetime, for example, but not the investments themselves. Neither the proper liferenter nor the liferent trust beneficiary has the right of ownership in the property concerned and so cannot sell or destroy the property. Where a proper liferent has been granted, the owner is referred to as the 'fiar' and the right of ownership as the 'fee'. In a liferent trust, the trustees own the property in question. Unlike an annuity, the duration of a liferent cannot be fixed by the testator. As the name suggests, liferent lasts for the lifetime of the holder. On the death of the liferenter, the owner is free to use the property as they wish, subject to any other terms which may be in place in a liferent trust.

Both an annuity and a liferent can be assigned by their holders to third parties. The exception to this rule is where the liferent is categorised as an alimentary liferent, designed to provide financially for the maintenance of a named person, usually a child of the testator.

Legatum rei alienae

Where the subject of the legacy is property which the testator did not own either at the time of execution of the will or on death, the bequest may be interpreted as a legacy *rei alienae* (meaning, roughly, a legacy of property belonging to another). A legacy of this type is understood to be an instruction from the testator to acquire the property bequeathed for the beneficiary. For this doctrine to come into play, the testator must have been aware that they did not own the property at the time of making the bequest, and the subject must be clearly ascertainable, following *Macfarlane's Trustees* v *Macfarlane* 1910 SC 325. For example, a bequest of 2,000 shares in Big PLC may be a legacy *rei alienae* if the testator was aware they did not own any such shares. However, a bequest of 'half my shares in Big PLC' cannot be a legacy *rei alienae* since it is impossible to ascertain how many shares the testator intended to bequeath.

Ademption

Ademption means cancellation. If the subject of a legacy does not form part of the testator's estate on death, it is assumed that the testator disposed of it deliberately. Disposal implies that the testator did not or no longer had the intention to bequeath the property, and in the absence of the necessary intention, that aspect of the will is considered to have been revoked.

A misdescription of the subject will not necessarily result in ademption. For example, if the Fender Telecaster guitar mentioned in the sample will was in fact a Fender Stratocaster, and the testator did not own any other guitars, it is likely that the legacy would be interpreted as a bequest of the Stratocaster (*Door* v *Geary* (1749) Vesey

Senior 132). If, however, the testator did not own any guitars, the legacy would adeem (meaning 'be cancelled').

Whether the subject of the legacy is part of the estate may not always be a straightforward question. The test to be applied is whether the substance of the bequest remains unchanged (*Stanley* v *Potter* (1789) 2 Cox Eq Cas 180). The case law on this point is not easy to reconcile. *Macfarlane's Trustees* v *Macfarlane* 1910 SC 325 found that where shares in a company were converted into stock in the same company, the essence of the property had not changed and so the legacy of the shares had not adeemed. However, in *Ballantyne's Trustees* v *Ballantyne's Trustees* 1941 SC 35, it was held that a legacy of money in a particular bank account adeemed where the money had been transferred into a different bank account.

Where heritable property is in the process of transfer from the testator to a third party, a legacy of that heritage will not adeem if the transfer is incomplete at the time of the testator's death. However, the beneficiary will inherit the property subject to the conditions placed on the testator's ownership of it at the time of their death (*McArthur's Executors* v *Guild* 1908 SC 743). For example, the subject of the legacy may be a house, in respect of which the testator had concluded missives and delivered a disposition at the time of their death. At this stage of the transaction, the seller of a house is under strict legal obligations not to do anything that will prevent the buyer from obtaining ownership of the house through registration of the title. The legacy of the house will vest in the beneficiary, but it is subject to the same obligations that bound the seller-testator, meaning the beneficiary cannot prevent the buyer from completing the sale transaction and acquiring ownership.

A testamentary writing will sometimes include an 'anti-ademption' clause. This allows the testator some freedom to continue dealing with their property during their lifetime without negating the provisions of the will. An example would be a legacy of 'my house at 12 Greenleaf Lane or such other heritable property as may be in my possession at the date of my death'. If the testator were to sell the house at Greenleaf Lane and buy another property, the bequest would not adeem. Rather, the subject of the legacy would become the testator's new house.

Abatement

Abatement means reduction. It may be the case that the property in the estate, after payment of debts and legal rights, is insufficient to pay all the legacies in full. In that case, some or all of the legacies will abate (be reduced). Abatement occurs in a specific order, with residual legacies abating first, followed by general legacies, demonstrative legacies and then specific legacies. In other words, specific legacies are paid in full first. Demonstrative legacies are paid in full provided the source of payment specified in the legacy allows for full payment to be made. General legacies are then paid in full. If there is anything left in the estate following payment of the general legacies, it will go to the residuary legatee(s).

Where there is more than one legacy within each of the categories, each will abate proportionately with the other legacies in that category. For example, if Victor has been left £100 and Wendy has been left £200 but only £150 remains in the estate, Victor will receive £50 and Wendy will receive £100. This rule will not apply to specific legacies, which cannot be proportionately reduced in this way.

The order of abatement can be altered by express provision in the will.

THE OBJECT OF A LEGACY

The object of a legacy is the person to whom the legacy has been left, also known as the legatee or the beneficiary. Difficulties can arise where the object of a legacy is not clearly identified.

Minor errors, such as a spelling mistake, in the identification of a beneficiary can be ignored so long as it is otherwise clear who was intended to receive the bequest. If there is doubt over the correct beneficiary, other information within the will may be used to resolve the uncertainty. In *Macfarlane's Trustees* v *Henderson* (1878) 6 R 288, a legacy was left to 'my late brother James's son'. The testator had a late brother James, who had a daughter, and also a surviving brother David, who had a son. The court considered it more likely that the testator would accidentally misgender his late brother's child than make a mistake in identifying his late brother, and so the legacy was payable to James's daughter. Where there is nothing in the will which helps to resolve the problem, extrinsic evidence may be permitted. In *Keiller* v *Thomson's Trustees* (1824) 3 S 279, the legacy was left to 'Janet Keiller or Williamson'. Was the legacy intended for Agnes Keiller/ Wedderspoon or Janet Keiller/Whitton? Evidence of earlier testamentary writings was admitted, in which Agnes Wedderspoon had frequently been the object of a similar legacy. The court concluded that Williamson was an erroneous transcription of Wedderspoon here.

Where a legatee is identified by reference to their relationship to another person, but that relationship no longer subsists by the time of the testator's death, the legacy may fail as a result. The wording of the testament will determine the outcome here in most cases, but the position is somewhat different for a spouse or civil partner of the testator. Section 1 of the Succession (Scotland) Act 2016 provides that where a legatee was the spouse or civil partner of the testator at the time the will was executed or later, but the marriage or civil partnership ended by divorce or dissolution prior to the testator's death, the will is to be interpreted as if the legatee had predeceased the testator. This changes the position under common law, where a spouse named as a legatee would continue to be a valid beneficiary even after divorce, which was considered to be out of step with what the public would expect to happen in this situation. A testator may nevertheless make express provision in their will to the effect that the legacy is to remain valid notwithstanding divorce or dissolution.

Where a legacy is made to a class of persons, such as the children or the siblings of the testator, certain presumptions apply. Unless the will provides otherwise, any person falling into the category at the time of the testator's death will be entitled to share in the legacy, even if they were not alive at the time the will was executed. Where the testator makes a bequest to 'children', it is only the immediate generation of descendants who are entitled to a share. Grandchildren or children of subsequent generations have no entitlement. Where the bequest is made to 'issue' rather than children, grandchildren and subsequent generations have an automatic entitlement to inherit the share their parent would have received, should their parent die before the testator. As an example, if a legacy is left to 'my friend Michael Wood's children', and only grandchildren of Michael Wood were alive at the time of the testator's death, they would not be entitled to claim and the legacy would fail. However, if the legacy had instead been to 'my friend Michael Wood's issue', the grandchildren could take the inheritance in the place of their parents.

If it is not possible to determine the identity of the object, the legacy will be void. The subject of the legacy will fall into the residue or, if it is the residuary legatee who cannot be identified, the residue of the estate will fall into intestacy.

DEATH OF A LEGATEE: DESTINATIONS

A legatee can only receive a legacy if they are alive when the testator dies. If the legatee predeceases the testator, generally speaking the legacy will fail. To avoid this result, the testator may include a **'destination-over'** in the legacy. This is a mechanism by which an alternative beneficiary can be specified in the event of the original legatee's predecease.

In a legacy with a destination-over, the original legatee will be known as the institute. Depending on the mechanism used, the alternative beneficiary will be called the conditional institute, or the substitute.

A **conditional institute** will inherit the legacy only if the institute predeceases the testator or fails to survive another event specified by the testator in the will. If the institute survives the testator or meets the condition specified, they will take the bequest in full, and the conditional institute will have no entitlement. So, imagine Alf leaves his car to Bella as the institute, whom failing to Cheryl as the conditional institute. If Bella dies before Alf, Cheryl will inherit the car. If Bella survives Alf, Bella will inherit the car, and Cheryl will receive nothing.

A **substitute** will inherit the legacy after the death of the institute, even where the institute survives the testator. So, imagine Alf has left his car to Bella as the institute and Cheryl as the substitute. If Bella predeceases Alf, Cheryl will inherit the car as before. If Bella survives Alf, Bella will inherit the car – but Cheryl does not lose out entirely, as she would do as a conditional institute. Cheryl as the substitute will be entitled to inherit the car *on Bella's death*. That is the effect of substitution.

The right of the substitute is not, however, as strong as it may first appear. This is because the institute is not bound to adhere to the testator's intention that the legacy should go to the substitute on the institute's death. Instead, the institute has the power to make alternative provision for the property in question, either by transferring ownership of the property to another party during their lifetime or by making a will in which the property is bequeathed to someone other than the substitute on the institute's death. This is known as **evacuating** the destination to the substitute. So, in the situation above where Cheryl is the substitute in respect of Bella's inheritance of Alf's car, Bella can evacuate the destination by selling the car during her lifetime or by making a will in which she leaves the car to Donald.

A will may clearly specify whether an alternative legatee is intended to be a conditional institute or a substitute. However common forms of wording, such as a legacy 'to A, whom failing B', do not indicate clearly which type of destination-over is intended. Where there is ambiguity, conditional institution is presumed under section 8 of the Succession (Scotland) Act 2016.

Where the testator wishes to include an **express** destination-over, the most common form of wording is 'to A, whom failing B'. The testator may also include a condition that the institute must survive him for a certain period of time, failing which B will inherit: 'to A, on the condition that he survive me for 30 days, whom failing B'.

If the testator has not included an express destination-over, in certain situations the law will **imply** one. Destinations-over will be implied in line with the doctrine of **accretion**, or where **section 6 of the Succession (Scotland) Act 2016** applies.

The doctrine of **accretion** may operate where a legacy has been left to more than one person, for example 'to A and B and C', or to a class of people, for example 'to the children of A and B'. Where one of the legatees dies before the testator, the law implies a destination-over in favour of the other legatees in that group. So if the will reads 'I leave £9,000 to A and B', this is understood to mean that A and B should share the money between them – but if one of them dies before the testator, then the survivor should inherit the whole £9,000. Another way of expressing this is to say that the predeceasing legatee's share in the legacy accresces to the surviving legatee(s).

Accretion can only operate where it is clear that the legacy was intended jointly, rather than severally, for the legatees. In other words, the testator intended that the property should be shared amongst however many people within the group of legatees survived the testator, rather than that intending a fixed share of the property should be available to each legatee alive at the time the will was executed. The testator's intentions in this respect may be clearly expressed in the will. If not, the law will assume a legacy is intended to be joint and therefore shared amongst whoever survives the testator *unless* words of severance are used. This rule was set out in *Paxton's Trustees* v *Cowie* (1886) 13 R 1191, where it was found that expressions such as 'equally among them', 'in equal shares', 'share and share alike' or anything with the same meaning would prevent the operation of accretion. So, where a legacy of £9,000 is left 'to A and B equally between them' and A dies before the testator, B nevertheless receives only half of the legacy. The share of the legacy intended for A fails, and that property falls into the residue.

Words of severance do not, however, prevent the operation of accretion where the legacy is left to a class of persons, such as 'my children equally among them' or 'the issue of A and B in equal shares'.

Section 6 of the Succession (Scotland) Act 2016 applies where the objects of the legacy are the direct descendants of the deceased, and one or more of those descendants was alive when the will was executed but died before the testator. If the predeceasing descendant has been survived by a child or children of their own, that child or those children will be entitled to take their parent's legacy unless it is clear from the terms of the will that the testator intended otherwise. The Act specifies that this intention will be clear if the legacy includes a destination-over or survivorship clause (discussed in Chapter 8), although these examples are not exhaustive. This provision replaced an older doctrine known as the *conditio si institutus sine liberis decesserit* which made wider provision for the descendants of a predeceasing legatee to inherit in their place. Section 29 of the 2016 Act provides that this doctrine ceases to have effect. Essentially the law now assumes that a testator would intend their own grandchildren to inherit but does not make the same assumption in respect of the children or grandchildren of other legatees.

Essential facts

- A will is composed principally of legacies which direct the executor in how to distribute the estate.

- General rules of contractual interpretation will apply to wills. The cardinal rule is that the will should be read in a way that gives effect to the testator's intentions.

- The subject of a legacy is the property bequeathed. Legacies can be categorised by subject as specific, demonstrative, general or residual legacies.

- If the legacy cannot be paid because the property is not or was never part of the testator's estate, it will adeem (be cancelled).

- If there is not enough in the estate to pay all the legacies in full, the legacies will abate (be reduced) in a particular order.

- The object of a legacy is the person to whom the legacy was left.

- The testator can create an alternative beneficiary to take the legacy if the original object dies. The alternative beneficiary may be a conditional institute, who will inherit if the original beneficiary dies before the testator, or a substitute, who will inherit *from* the original beneficiary after they die.

- Destinations-over can also be created by implication through the doctrine of accretion where the legacy is left to a group of people, or through the operation of section 6 of the Succession (Scotland) Act 2016, which allows the testator's grandchildren to inherit in place of their parents in certain circumstances.

Essential cases

Macfarlane's Trustees v Macfarlane 1910 SC 325: The deceased had owned shares in a company and made a will leaving the shares to his mother and sisters. A few months before his death, the deceased became incapable of managing his own affairs, and a curator bonis was appointed to look after them. The curator sold the shares. Did the legacy therefore adeem? The court considered that action taken by a curator could not impact on the deceased's testamentary provision unless it was a necessary and unavoidable act on the curator's part. The shares had been sold in this case simply because the curator considered it prudent to do so. Accordingly, the legacy did not adeem, and the beneficiaries were entitled to receive the value of the shares from the estate.

FURTHER READING

A Barr, A Dalgleish and H Stevens, *Drafting Wills in Scotland* (2nd ed, 2009), chapters 3–6

Hiram, *Succession*, chapters 8 and 9

Macdonald, *Succession*, chapter 10

D R Macdonald, "Lapse of legacies" in E Cooke (ed) *Modern Studies in Property Law: Volume 1* (2001)

SAMPLE WILL

This is one possible example of how a formally valid will could be written. The contents of the sample will are set out in a different font to the rest of the book. Commentary on the will, which would not form part of the document, is written in italicised font within square brackets *[like this]*.

WILL

I, LOGAN ROY residing at One University Square, Hillhead, Glasgow, G12 3AB in order to settle the succession to my estate after my death provide as follows:

(ONE) I revoke all prior Wills and testamentary writings. *[This is known as a 'revocation clause'.]*

(TWO) I appoint LAW AND SONS LIMITED, a Company incorporated under the Companies Act 2006 (Company Number ABC123) and having its Registered Office at Three University Street, Glasgow and JOCELYN PARKER SINGH, residing at Fourteen The Cinnamons, Wester Broughtynoustie, to be my Executors. *[The testator has nominated a law firm and an individual to act as his executors. The final clause of the will sets out the powers the executors will be entitled to exercise.]*

(THREE) I direct my Executors to make over the sum of THREE HUNDRED POUNDS (£300) STERLING to my son, KENDALL ROY residing at Four Willow Crescent, Stirling. *[This is a general legacy.]*

(FOUR) I direct my Executors to make over my Fender Telecaster electric guitar to THOMAS WAMBSGANS residing at Fifteen Oak Lane, Perth whom failing to GREGORY HIRSCH residing at Twenty Birch Avenue, Elgin. *[This is a specific legacy. Thomas Wambsgans is the institute and Gregory Hirsch is the alternative beneficiary. The wording of the legacy does not make clear whether Gregory is intended to be a conditional institute or a substitute, so conditional institution will be presumed.]*

(FIVE) I direct my Executors to make over one half of my shares in APPLE RECORDS PLC to FRANK VERNON also residing at Twenty Birch Avenue, Elgin and HUGO BAKER residing at Eight Pine Street,

Oban equally between them. *[This is a specific legacy. The words of severance – 'equally between them' – prevent accretion from operating in respect of the legacy. This means that if Frank predeceases the testator, his half of the legacy will not go to Hugo. Instead, it will fall into the residue.]*

(SIX) I direct my Executors to make over the sum of FIVE HUNDRED POUNDS (£500) STERLING to GREENPEACE, (REGISTERED CHARITY NUMBER SC12345).

(SEVEN) I direct my Executors to make over the residue of my estate to my daughter SIOBHAN ROY residing at Three Elm Gardens, Hillhead, Glasgow. In the event of the said Siobhan Roy failing to survive me I direct my Executors to make over the residue to my son ROMAN ROY residing at Thirteen Poplar Crescent, Hillhead, Glasgow. *[Siobhan is the residuary legatee. It is clear from the wording of the legacy that Roman is intended to be a conditional institute, not a substitute.]*

(LASTLY) My Executors shall have the fullest powers of retention, realisation, investment, appropriation, transfer of property without realisation, and management of my estate as if they were absolute beneficial owners; and they shall have power to resign office and to appoint solicitors or agents in any other capacity from amongst their own number or from the said Law and Sons Limited and to allow him, her, it or them the remuneration to which he, she, it or they would ordinarily be entitled: IN WITNESS WHEREOF these presents consisting of this and the one preceding page are executed as follows:

THEY ARE SUBSCRIBED BY ME, the said

LOGAN ROY

at THREE UNIVERSITY STREET, GLASGOW

on the THIRD

day of MAY

in the year TWO THOUSAND AND TWENTY FOUR subscribing my usual signature before this witness, namely: *[The words from IN*

WITNESS WHEREOF to here make up the testing clause, narrating the circumstances of the subscription and witnessing of the will.]

L Roy *[Standard method of signature.]*

Witness: Gerri Kellman

Gerri Kellman

23 Main Street

Edinburgh

EH1 2AB

Solicitor *[The occupation of the witness is usually stated.]*

8 WILL SUBSTITUTES

It is possible for a person to make some provision for the distribution of their property on death without writing a will. Other forms of testamentary device – referred to here as 'will substitutes' – remain popular and, particularly where the estate is relatively modest, it may be more efficient to make provision in this way. This chapter will consider the two main forms of will substitute, namely **special destinations** and **nominations**.

Section 36(2) of the Succession (Scotland) Act 1964 provides that property disposed of by means of a will substitute does not form part of the estate on death. Accordingly, this property is not available to satisfy prior or legal rights claims.

SPECIAL DESTINATIONS, INCLUDING SURVIVORSHIP DESTINATIONS

A special destination is a clause in the deed of title to property which sets out who should obtain ownership of the property on the death of the current owner. The word 'special' denotes that the destination relates to this specific piece of property and no other. Special destinations can be created only where the property in question has a written title, meaning they are most commonly employed in relation to heritage in respect of which written title is a requirement. A written title for moveable property is encountered less frequently, but special destinations are sometimes inserted into share certificates and insurance policies.

A **survivorship clause** is the most familiar form of special destination. It is used in respect of property owned in common between two or more people, each of whom wishes on their death for their share in the property to transfer to the co-owners. Where a husband and wife co-own a house, title may be held by 'Gail and Henry and the survivor of them'. If Gail dies before Henry, her half-share of ownership of the house will automatically pass into his patrimony, meaning that he will own the whole house. If Henry dies first, Gail will become the owner.

The inclusion of a survivorship destination in a title does not prevent the owner from dealing with the property, or their share in the property, during their lifetime. The owner may sell or donate the property, for example, and the intended beneficiary of the survivorship clause cannot veto or otherwise prevent the transaction taking place. Where the granter of the survivorship destination disposes of the relevant property during their life, preventing the destination from taking effect, this is referred to as 'evacuating' the destination.

A survivorship destination can also be evacuated on death if the granter of the destination has made alternative testamentary provision for the property in question subsequent to the date of the destination. Section 30 of the Succession (Scotland) Act 1964 sets out requirements for evacuation in this way. The testamentary writing must explicitly refer to the survivorship destination and state expressly the testator's intention to evacuate it. General provision that a will revokes all prior testamentary writings will not suffice, since a special destination is not a testamentary writing. The testator must also have power to evacuate the destination. *Brown's Trustee* v *Brown* 1943 SC 488 confirmed that where one person has paid the full purchase price for a property which is nevertheless owned in common between two people, the person who provided the funds has the power to evacuate a survivorship destination in that title by subsequent testamentary writing. *Perrett's Trustees* v *Perrett* 1909 SC 522 found that where both parties had contributed equally to the purchase price, an implied contract existed between them that neither would evacuate the survivorship destination, and so any contrary testamentary provision could be set aside.

Section 2 of the Succession (Scotland) Act 2016 provides that where a survivorship destination is included in the title to property owned in common by spouses or civil partners, and the marriage or civil partnership is terminated by divorce, dissolution or annulment, the destination is impliedly revoked by each party being deemed to have predeceased the other. This provision effectively allows the termination of the relationship to evacuate any special destination, rather than evacuation being effected through transfer of the property or appropriate testamentary provision. If parties do not wish this provision to apply, they can provide expressly to that effect when drafting the destination.

Although property subject to a special destination does not form part of the estate, it is nevertheless available for satisfaction of the rights of creditors, which must be paid before any other claims on the estate. This rule, confirmed in *Fleming's Trustees* v *Fleming* 2000 SLT 406, is explained by the fact that the substitute cannot take a greater right than that held by the institute. Since the deceased's ownership was subject to the rights of creditors, the survivor's ownership must be similarly encumbered.

NOMINATION

A less common form of will substitute is a nomination. Statute provides that the holders of accounts with certain financial institutions, principally friendly societies, can nominate a person to receive any funds remaining in the account on their death. The nomination takes effect like a special destination, with funds vesting immediately in the nominee rather than in the executor. Revocation of the nomination is possible only by following the procedure set out in statute: as with special destinations, a clause in a will revoking prior testamentary writings will not affect a nomination. The current statutory provisions allowing for disposal of property on death by nomination are listed in Schedule 2 to the Administration of Estates (Small Payments) Act 1965. The 1965 Act also limits the amount of money in one account capable of disposal by nomination to £5,000.

The proceeds of a life insurance policy may pass to a nominated beneficiary in much the same way and will accordingly not form part of the deceased's estate. If no beneficiary has been named, and the proceeds are to be paid to the deceased's executors, they will form part of the estate in the usual way. A third alternative is that the policy may have been taken by the deceased in trust for their spouse or children. Such an arrangement will be regulated by the Married Women's Policies of Assurance (Scotland) Act 1880, which has been amended to apply to any married person or civil partner. If the policy specifies that it is being held in trust for the spouse and/or children, the proceeds will again pass directly to the beneficiary without vesting in the executors.

DONATION *MORTIS CAUSA*

Until the introduction of the Succession (Scotland) Act 2016, a third form of will substitute known as donation *mortis causa* was available. This involved the testator making a lifetime donation of property to a beneficiary, subject to a condition that the donation could be revoked at any point prior to the testator's death. This mechanism caused difficulties in practice, not least that it was not always clear whether a donation of property was conditional or unconditional. Donation *mortis causa* was abolished by section 25 of the 2016 Act.

Essential facts

A will substitute allows a person to make provision for their property on death without making a will.

- A special destination is a clause in the deed of title to property specifying who should inherit that property on the owner's death.
- A special destination providing that a predeceasing co-owner's share of ownership is to go to the remaining co-owner(s) is known as a survivorship destination.
- Special destinations can be evacuated by lifetime disposal of the property or express testamentary provision in certain cases. A special destination to a spouse or civil partner will be deemed revoked by termination of the relationship.
- Limited amounts of money held in accounts with certain non-mainstream financial institutions can be left to another person by nomination. The proceeds of a life insurance policy can also be inherited in this way.

Essential cases

Perrett's Trustees v Perrett 1909 SC 522: The deceased made a will revoking all prior testamentary writings. The estate included the deceased's share of heritable property owned in common with his surviving spouse. Each had contributed one-half of the purchase price, and the title was held by each of them and to the survivor of them. Had this special destination in favour of the deceased's wife been evacuated by the will? The court considered that since the property was heritable and both spouses had contributed one-half of the price, the destination was contractual in nature, with each spouse agreeing to take the chance of inheriting the other spouse's share. Since a contract cannot be altered by one of the parties acting unilaterally, it was not possible for survivorship destination to be evacuated by the deceased's will.

Fleming's Trustees v Fleming 2000 SLT 406: A husband and wife owned a house between them and to the survivor of them. The husband had been sequestrated ("went bankrupt') and subsequently died. Was his half share of the house, which passed to his wife on his death by virtue of the survivorship destination, subject to the claims of his creditors? The court held that it was. His wife, as his substitute, could not hold a better right than the deceased had. His share in the house was subject to the claims of his creditors, and accordingly the creditors had the right to enforce those claims against his wife up to the value of his share in the property.

FURTHER READING

DJ Carr, "Will substitutes in Scotland" in A Braun and A Röthel (eds) *Passing Wealth on Death: Will-Substitutes in Comparative Perspective* (2016)

Hiram, *Succession*, paragraphs 2.10–2.23

Macdonald, *Succession*, chapter 5

9 VESTING

Following the death of a testator, a legacy is sometimes said to 'vest' in the beneficiary. In this context, what this means is that the legatee has an indefeasible right to acquire ownership of the legacy. However, they have not yet acquired ownership, or even possession, of the property bequeathed to them in the will.

The concept of vesting plays a role at various stages in the succession process. The estate vests in the executor at the moment confirmation is granted. Legal rights to an intestate estate vest at the point of the intestate's death. The right of a legatee under a will vests at the moment of the testator's death, or at some later stage if that is provided for in the will.

WHAT IS A VESTED RIGHT?

A vested right to a piece of property is not the same as ownership. Rather, it is a personal right to have that property transferred or paid to the holder of the vested right in due course.

Like other personal rights, a vested right can be assigned to another person or included within the holder's will. This can be important where a will provides that payment of a legacy is postponed until a certain time. For example, Imran's will might leave a legacy of £5,000 to Julie, not to be paid until Julie is 21, whom failing to Karl. Imran dies when Julie is 18. At this stage, the right to payment of the legacy vests in Julie, although that right cannot be exercised until she turns 21. Julie then dies at the age of 19. Since the right to the £5,000 is already vested in Julie, it is part of her estate on death. The right to the money will therefore pass on to Julie's heirs. It will *not* pass to Karl. Karl would only have taken the legacy if Julie had died *before Imran*. Since Julie survived Imran, the legacy had already vested in her.

WHEN DO RIGHTS IN SUCCESSION VEST?

Rights that arise on intestacy vest at the point of death. Rights arising under a will are more complicated, however, since the testator has the power to determine the time at which the legacy vests. The earliest point at which a right can vest is on the testator's death. The latest point is the date when payment of the legacy falls due.

The point at which vesting should occur may be clearly expressed in the will. However, ambiguity can arise as to the testator's intentions in this regard. The law has set out a series of rules which will operate to determine the testator's intentions where they are not clearly expressed. The general rules on interpretation of wills apply, meaning that the ultimate goal of the law here is to ascertain the testator's true intention. There is a presumption against an interpretation that will result in intestacy. In the absence of anything to suggest the contrary, it will be presumed that the legacy was intended to vest at the earliest possible date, which is the date of the testator's death. If the wording of the will clearly excludes that interpretation, the next presumption is that vesting was intended to be postponed until the date of payment. The wording of the will itself may overturn this presumption also, however.

VESTING OF CONDITIONAL LEGACIES

Legacies may sometimes be subject to conditions, as discussed in Chapter 7. For example, Imran might leave a legacy of £5,000 to Liam provided he is still in full time education. The requirement that Liam is still a student is a condition of his inheritance. If he fulfils (or 'purifies' in the legal terminology) the condition, he will receive the legacy. If he does not, the legacy will pass to an alternative legatee or fall into the residue. It is as if Imran had left the legacy to a person who does not exist. No person called Liam in full time education existed at the point of Imran's death, and so the legacy would be treated as it would in any situation where the legatee had failed, as discussed in Chapter 7.

The effect of the condition attached to a legacy on vesting will depend on how it is expressed. The condition may relate simply to payment of the legacy, as with Julie's legacy of £5,000 not to be paid until she reached 21. In that case, the legacy will vest at the point of the testator's death as usual.

Alternatively, the condition may be a requirement of the inheritance itself, rather than simply a question of the timing of payment. The condition that Liam still be in full time education is an example. In Liam's case, the condition was not fulfilled at the point of the testator's death, so the legacy did not vest.

Conditions may also relate to future events in the lives of legatees. A legacy may be left to Miriam provided she reaches the age of 18. Unlike Julie, this is not simply a delay in payment. Miriam must reach the age of 18 or she has no right to the legacy. How does a future condition of this kind impact on vesting? The law draws a distinction between future events which will definitely happen, known as *dies certus*, and future events which may or may not ever happen, known as *dies incertus*. The most obvious example of a *dies certus* is death, since everyone will die at some point. Common examples of *dies incertus* include the marriage of a person, or a person attaining a particular age. Where the condition attached to the legacy is a *dies certus*, the legacy vests immediately at the point of death, since the future event will definitely happen. A *dies certus* condition is essentially just a delay in payment. However, where the condition is a *dies incertus*, the legacy cannot vest unless and until the uncertain event actually happens. Conditions of this kind are sometimes described as suspensive conditions, since vesting is postponed unless and until the condition is purified.

An example may help to illustrate the difference. Imran may leave a legacy of £5,000 to Nick on his mother's death, and another legacy of £5,000 to Orla on the birth of her first child. Nick's mother is inevitably going to die at some point, so that legacy will vest in Nick at the point of Imran's death. However, Orla may or may not ever have children. The legacy to Orla cannot vest in her until the point at which her first child is born.

Why is it important whether the legacy has vested or not? Nick cannot obtain the money until his mother dies; Orla cannot obtain the money until she has a child. Whether or not the legacy has vested beforehand would seem to make no practical difference. In so far as it affects Nick and Orla directly, this is largely correct, although Nick may assign his vested right to someone else if he so chooses, for whatever that might be worth, an option not open to Orla. However, the question of vesting becomes most significant for Nick and Orla's heirs. If Nick dies before his mother does, he will not have been able to obtain the money left to him by Imran at any point during his lifetime. However, the right to the legacy had already vested in him. It therefore forms part of his estate and will be inherited in turn by his heirs. Conversely, if Orla dies before she has had a child, no right to the money from Imran has ever vested in her, and her heirs will not be entitled to that legacy.

Ascertaining whether the testator intended to impose a suspensive condition or simply to suspend payment of the legacy is not always an easy task. A common form of wording may be 'to Poppy on turning 40'. Is this a suspensive condition, indicating that Poppy is to receive the legacy only if she reaches 40? Or is it intended that the legacy should vest on the testator's death with payment suspended until Poppy's 40th birthday? The case law on interpretation of legacies of this type is complex and possibly conflicting. Detailed discussion can be found in the further reading listed at the end of this chapter.

One common situation in which there is a question as to whether a condition postpones vesting or simply postpones payment is where the legacy contains a survivorship clause. Imagine that Imran leaves a legacy to his nieces Ruby, Rose and Rachel and the survivor of them, to be paid on their mother's death. What is the event beyond which the nieces must survive before the legacy will vest in them? Their mother's death is a *dies certus*, so under the rules outlined above, vesting should occur at the point of Imran's death. In that case, it would seem to follow that the nieces need only survive until the moment of Imran's death, at which time the legacy will vest, with payment suspended until their mother dies. However, the law does not take this approach. In *Young* v *Robertson* (1862) 4 Macq 314 the court set out the presumption that survivance should be taken, as a general rule of construction, to refer to the date of payment of a legacy.

DEFEASIBLE VESTING

In a limited number of situations, the law will allow a legacy to be subject to a resolutive condition. A resolutive condition is in some sense the opposite of a suspensive condition: it means that the legacy vests in the legatee *unless and until* the specific event occurs. The usual example is that a legacy will vest unless and until a named person has children, in which case the legacy should go to the children instead.

The law in this area is again complex. However, in general, a resolutive condition can only be attached to a legacy in which payment has been suspended. The justification for this may be largely pragmatic: if the legacy vests and is paid immediately to the legatee, how can they be made to repay in the event that the resolutive condition is purified?

Most commonly a resolutive condition will be placed on a legacy of property which has been left to one party in liferent, and a second party in fee. A liferent is a real right entitling the holder to make use of the property in which the right is held for the duration of their lifetime. The fee is ownership of that property subject to the liferent. Imran might leave his house to Sophie in liferent and Tom in fee. This would allow Sophie to live in Imran's house for the remainder of Sophie's life, although Tom will be the owner of it. In such a situation, Imran might apply a resolutive condition to the legacy to Tom, saying that he is to take in fee unless Sophie has children, in which case the children are to be preferred. At the point at which Imran dies, the liferent vests in Sophie and the fee vests in Tom. If Sophie has a child, the fee comes out of Tom's patrimony and vests instead in Sophie's child.

Essential facts

- Where a legacy vests in a beneficiary, they have an indefeasible personal right to obtain ownership of that property. In the succession context, the right is usually held against the executor of the estate.

- Rights arising on intestacy will vest in the beneficiaries at the moment when the intestate dies.

- A testator may specify when rights arising under a will should vest. The earliest point at which vesting can occur is on the testator's death. The latest point is on the date when payment is due.
- A legacy subject to a *dies certus* condition, such as a death, will vest in the beneficiary immediately on the testator's death. A legacy subject to a *dies incertus* condition, such as a marriage, will not vest unless and until the condition is fulfilled.

FURTHER READING

R Candlish Henderson, *The Principles of Vesting in the Law of Succession* (2nd ed, 1938)
Macdonald, *Succession*, chapter 11

10 FUTURE DEVELOPMENTS

DIFFICULT QUESTIONS

The previous chapters have explained that the law of succession does several things: it provides the technical rules that govern how and when property can pass from a person who has died to another person; it places constraints on a person's testamentary freedom including through the entitlement of any surviving spouse and children to legal rights; and it supplies a set of default rules that determine who will inherit property when the deceased has not made valid testamentary provision to that effect.

Succession, like most areas of law, does not stand still. Changes are required to reflect developments in societal expectations and beliefs. Unlike some areas of law, though, succession tends to change very slowly. This is particularly the case in relation to aspects of succession law where societal consensus about the appropriate rules is difficult to achieve, for example in relation to the protection of certain family members from disinheritance or as regards the default rules on intestacy.

Consider your own views on the following questions: should a person be free to disinherit their spouse or children? If not, what should a spouse or child be entitled to receive from the estate? Should a cohabitant of the deceased have the same entitlement as a spouse? Who should be entitled to inherit the estate of a person who has not left a will? Are there any circumstances in which a person should be barred from inheriting? If you try to answer those questions and then ask a friend what their answers would be, you might well discover that your answers will be different.

Disagreements on the law of succession may have their roots in the different beliefs or values adhered to by different members of society. Some people ascribe to the view that a person should be free to do what they want with their own property on death, perhaps subject to exceptions where dependents would be left in need if they did not inherit. Other people consider there to be an ethical or moral obligation on every person to provide for their family on death, which is arguably a continuation of the expectation that family members will look after each other in life. Inheritance may also be viewed as a cause of increasing wealth inequality within our society, leading some to call for more stringent limits on how much property a person can leave to others on their death. The views of any individual are likely to depend to some extent on their own experiences, and the views they express may depend on how the question has been asked.

The diversity of views on succession within current Scottish society has made it difficult for legislators to carry out reform to the law in recent years. Many are critical of the current rules on legal rights and intestate succession, and it is generally accepted that the rules could be improved, but there is no agreement on how.

There have been several recent attempts to reform the law, some of which are discussed in more detail in the following paragraphs. The attempts at reform began with the Scottish Law Commission's Report in 1990, which recommended major changes to large parts of succession including a replacement for legal rights. The Report did not lead to any immediate changes. The SLC produced a further Report on succession in 2009, which repeated some of the recommendations made in the earlier Report and made some new recommendations, to some extent reflecting the changes in society in the intervening period. The Succession (Scotland) Act 2016 implemented some of these recommendations, as discussed in earlier chapters. The 2009 Report again recommended a replacement for legal rights and changes to the intestate succession regime, but again these recommendations were not taken forward. In 2015, the Scottish Government carried out an extensive public consultation on aspects of succession law addressed by the SLC in their Reports. The responses received suggested there was no clear consensus on how the law should be reformed. A further consultation in 2019 moved matters no further forward. The government have committed to more targeted consultation in future. Below, we consider some areas where reform is under consideration, although it remains unclear when (or if) any reform will take place.

SPOUSES AND COHABITANTS

At present, the rights of cohabitants are restricted to claims on intestacy. A person who has been in a long-term cohabiting relationship with the deceased, resembling in every way what people might expect from a marriage, might nevertheless find themselves with nothing if the deceased has made no provision for them in a will. This may be perceived as unfair. In its 2009 Report, the Scottish Law Commission recommended (paras 4.9 and 4.21) that a new set of rules be introduced so that cohabitants could claim a percentage of the estate both from testate and intestate estates. Subsequent government consultation has not resulted in a clear view from the public of whether this change is desirable. It is likely that further consultation by government on changes to the succession regime for cohabitants will take place in the next few years.

FREEDOM OF TESTATION, DISINHERITANCE AND INTESTACY

More contentious still is what the law should do where a person has made a will which excludes their surviving spouse or child. Viewed from the perspective of the testator, any rules which protect a spouse or child from disinheritance are a restraint on the freedom to test which is generally a strong principle in our law. Viewed from the perspective of the spouse or child, these rules may be considered to provide essential financial protection in the face of a bereavement. It follows that the law must strike some sort of balance, but the question is where that balance is most appropriately struck. A similar issue arises in relation to the rules applicable where a person has not left a valid will, where the concern is to strike the right balance between the interests of different persons surviving the deceased.

Various proposals for reform of our current rules on legal rights and intestacy have been formulated in recent decades, by the Scottish Law Commission in their 1990 and 2009 Reports and separately by the Scottish Government in 2015 and 2019. The proposed rules suggest different ways of distributing intestate estates. All the proposed schemes to date reject total testamentary freedom and incorporate provisions intended to protect surviving spouses and children from disinheritance.

In the 1990 Report, the Scottish Law Commission recommended (2.7) that where a person died intestate survived by a spouse and children then the spouse should receive a fixed share and any surplus should be divided half to the spouse and half to the children. Legal rights were to be replaced by 'legal shares', which were fixed percentages of the estate as a whole. By 2009, the position of the Scottish Law Commission had evolved. This Report proposed similar changes to intestate succession, but proposed a more limited regime of legal shares. After consulting on the 2009 Report proposals, the Scottish Government, in their own consultation in 2019, suggested yet further alternative rules drawing on regimes in place in the province of British Columbia in Canada and the state of Washington in the USA (2.23 onwards). The consultation illustrates the benefits to lawmakers of considering how other jurisdictions deal with problems that must be addressed by every national legal system. However, it did not produce a clear consensus from the public on reform. Again, further consultation by government on these issues is anticipated in the next few years.

WILL-MAKING: FORMAL VALIDITY

The requirements for formal validity of a will are outlined in Chapter 6 of this book. These requirements were brought into focus by the COVID-19 pandemic when it was not always possible, or at least not easy, for the testator to sign their will in the presence of a witness. For a short period, the requirement that the testator and the witness be physically present when the will was signed was waived, and signature and witnessing by video call was permitted. While that was a relatively minor change in response to an extraordinary situation, it was a reminder that technology has moved on considerably since the 1995 Act came into force. Many documents now exist only in digital form. When it comes to wills, the approach to formal validity has tended to be quite conservative (for example, the requirement that each page of a will be signed). However, it seems likely that steps will have to be taken to allow for the creation of entirely digital wills in the near future.

WILL-MAKING AND PUBLIC PERCEPTIONS

There is little empirical research on wills and what the public think will happen to their estates when they die. The research which does exist (for example, Scottish Consumer Council, *Wills and Awareness of Inheritance Rights in Scotland*, 2006) suggests that most people do not have a will and that many people do not have an accurate understanding of the rules of intestacy. These findings might suggest that the present regime does not align with societal expectations and might also suggest that the present regime is too complicated. In either case, it seems inarguable that public education on these aspects of the law should be improved. Whether there is any progress on this issue in the near future, whether by way of government action or otherwise, remains to be seen.

Essential facts

- Succession law affects everyone, but it affects them differently.
- Governments have to make rules considering (i) the right of a person to dispose of their estate as they wish and (ii) the rights of those left behind to inherit that estate.
- Governments also have to make rules determining who will inherit the estate of a person who has not left a valid will.
- In many cases, the solution to succession problems can be (or could have been) solved by a person leaving a valid will.

FURTHER READING

Scottish Government, *Consultation on the Law of Succession* (2015) available at https://consult.gov.scot/civil-law-reform-unit/consultation-on-the-law-of-succession/

Scottish Government, *Consultation on the Law of Succession* (2019) available at https://www.gov.scot/publications/consultation-law-succession/

Scottish Law Commission, *Report on Succession* (Scot Law Com No 124) (1990)

Scottish Law Commission, *Report on Succession* (Scot Law Com No 215) (2009)

INDEX